Library of Congress Cataloging-in-Publication Data
Names: Hogan, Ginny, author.
Title: I'm more dateable than a plate of refried beans : and other romantic observations / by Ginny Hogan.
Description: San Francisco : Chronicle Books, [2022]
Identifiers: LCCN 2021031784 | ISBN 9781797212265 (hardcover) |
Subjects: LCSH: Dating (Social customs)--Humor. |
Online dating--Humor. | Man-woman relationships--Humor. |
Single people--Humor.
Classification: LCC HQ801 .H674 2022 | DDC 306.73--dc23
LC record available at https://lccn.loc.gov/2021031784

Manufactured in China.

Design by Maggie Edelman.

Cover art by Nubia Navarro.

10 9 8 7 6 5 4 3 2 1

Chronicle Books LLC
680 Second Street
San Francisco, CA 94107
www.chroniclebooks.com

·I'M MORE· DATEABLE THAN A PLATE OF Refried Beans AND OTHER ROMANTIC ·OBSERVATIONS·

By Ginny Hogan

CHRONICLE BOOKS
SAN FRANCISCO

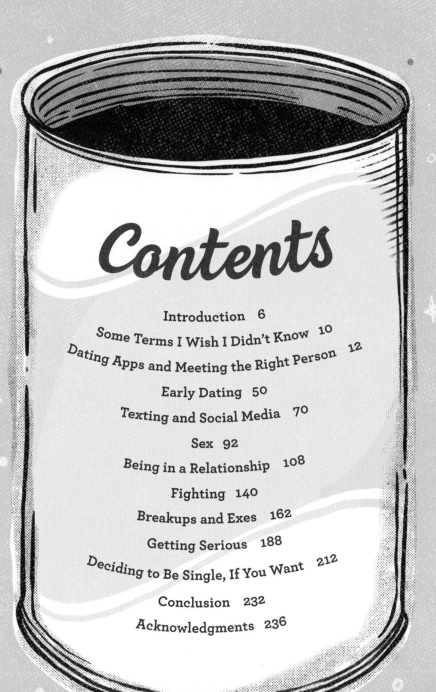

Contents

Introduction 6

Some Terms I Wish I Didn't Know 10

Dating Apps and Meeting the Right Person 12

Early Dating 50

Texting and Social Media 70

Sex 92

Being in a Relationship 108

Fighting 140

Breakups and Exes 162

Getting Serious 188

Deciding to Be Single, If You Want 212

Conclusion 232

Acknowledgments 236

Introduction

....

I once spent fifteen minutes telling my mother about a serious conflict at my job—I couldn't figure out how to adjust the height of my chair. She suggested I try the lever on the left and, as usual, she was correct. After I unloaded my professional anxieties for another fifteen minutes, she asked, "Are you having any fun, though? Like, are you dating?"

I had to ask her to repeat the question. I was confused. It had never occurred to me that dating was supposed to be *fun*.

When I was fifteen, I lied to the general public (my two friends) and said I'd kissed a boy I hadn't. When I was sixteen, I lied again and said I hadn't kissed a boy I had. When I was seventeen, I got my first boyfriend, thereby marking the official "launch" of my love life. Since then, it's gotten a bit out of hand, spanning whole months of five OkCupid dates a week, serious relationships, monogamy, nonmonogamy, nonmonogamy I believed was monogamy, dumping, getting dumped, six months (or eleven, depending on how you count) of celibacy, watching a man leave mid-sex to eat peanut butter, eating peanut butter mid-sex myself (same guy, we were together a while), drunkenly sleeping around every night, getting sober and relearning the basics of dating, another six months of celibacy, falling for someone I'd never met IRL, meeting someone in the middle of a pandemic, and sharing every last ghastly experience with my closest friends and Twitter followers. I once even quit dating altogether, in a strategic move that was met with little to no resistance from the male community. It's been exhausting, but at least I had peanut butter.

It doesn't help my fatigue that dating has been turned on its head in the last decade. (My mother once recommended that on first dates, I ask the person, "What does IPA stand for?" That's honestly genius—how did she know that nothing hooks a man like the opportunity to talk about beer or, more importantly, facts that he knows?) But in general, aside from men loving to talk about themselves, dating is completely different than it was a generation ago. We're playing a brand-new game in which people are all too quick to hide behind their phones, invent their own rules of civility, and fear any sort of stability. My mom is unfamiliar with the swiping and the ghosting and the breadcrumbing and crumb-bedding and the way you can devote seventeen concentrated hours to analyzing why your crush chose to like your Instagram pic of a pancake but not the one of French toast (perhaps because the circle is an inherently sexual shape?). And I often feel too silly to explain any of these phenomena to her. As I should.

I grew up during a pivotal time for the way we approach dating and relationships. I graduated from an all-girls high school in 2009, the year Obama took office, Circuit City went out of business, and Paris Hilton dazzled us by double-fisting two bejeweled BlackBerry handheld devices. The year 2009 was a transitional year for phones—flip phones weren't quite out of date and smartphones were still thrilling enough that we weren't yet at the point of regularly vowing to throw them into the sea. My freshman year of college, I got my first iPhone *and* my first daily dose of boys, so I had to learn how to text and date simultaneously. It was like trying to shampoo your hair and brush your teeth at the same time. Don't try it, no matter how busy you are—you will eat shampoo.

It's impossible to discuss modern dating without deliberating over our phones—a luxury that quickly became a burden. I've been so frustrated by my phone that I've resorted to drastic actions, such as not using my phone for twenty minutes. I direct as much anger and frustration toward my phone and its myriad apps as toward any of the people I date. There were times where I snapped my SIM card in half to get off my phone. There were times where I woke up after a night of drunk-texting to a message that read, "Thanks for the novel." There were times where I texted a guy that I liked him and then immediately blocked his number. I really can't defend this behavior. I once saw a toddler knock over a bowl of M&Ms with his Buzz Lightyear doll, and then explain that it was Buzz who did the damage, not him. That's how I feel about my phone.

The device that enables me to find new romantic options in a matter of minutes is the same one that enables my self-sabotage again, and again, and again. It's hard to install and uninstall Hinge eight times *in the same day* without wondering if I've done something wrong. And if you've never felt the same way, I'd encourage you to keep it to yourself, because it's not relatable.

I was single for most of my twenties, and I can't pretend I never felt like that meant I was failing. I've always taken a goal-oriented approach to dating, and by my own standards, I wasn't achieving my goals. In my mind, the end goal of dating wasn't to have a good time, it was to find a person to spend my time with, deliberately, forever, without fear that they'd ever leave me. And if I hadn't found that person when everyone else had, what had I been doing wrong? I'd see my friends in relationships and start to feel jealous, even if their partners were the type of people who leave voicemails when they could just send a text (this is an objectively unhinged thing to do; please just text). I felt competitive, and for what? Dating isn't a zero-sum game. It's possible for everyone to lose.

When I'm in nice relationships, I don't experience the sustained and elevated joy the movies misled me to think I'd feel. The phrase "happily ever after" should be amended to "potentially mentally okay, assuming both people continue working on themselves and probably go to therapy." With any new relationship comes the onset of fear about the breakup—I now have something I *really* don't want to lose.

When I'm single, the whole dating thing feels futile. I've wasted hundreds, if not thousands, of evenings trying to impress people I don't even talk to anymore. I even found that I had a lot more fun when I was committed to being single. I went to weddings alone in my early and mid-twenties and had a good time. I went to weddings alone in my late twenties and still had a good time (depending on the cake), but I started to wonder if my turn would come. And, if I was having fun by myself, did I even want it to?

As a woman who has bravely hit the other side of twenty-five, I've witnessed the dating conversation among my friends transition from funny anecdotes to serious discussions about how to "settle down" and start a family. This goes way over my head—sure, I may buy a house, start a family, own several horses, and commit to being in the same place for decades. But something about the words "settle down" makes me feel like I'll stop changing, or converge on some sort of "normal." That strikes me as unlikely.

Partnering up isn't the road to stability it used to be. With medical advances, more and more people are moving forward with having kids without a romantic partner. With rising divorce rates, marriage no longer provides the stability it used to. So, then, is the point of dating to have fun? If so, it fails. Is it to learn? Read a book! Read this one.

But there's a reason we keep mounting the dating horse (a metaphor—get your mind out of the gutter) again, and again, and again, even after our date told us we looked like "Elizabeth Holmes if she didn't try" (I try). Because every once in a while, it's pretty nice, even if it's brief and distracting and ultimately heartbreaking.

So if I'm going to repeat this cycle over and over again—as you might, too—I may as well try to have fun. You don't have to be swiping daily to take a step back and peer with amusement upon this strange institution we've invented. No matter where you stand—in a relationship, actively dating, happily single, Emma Watson, or anywhere in between—you can still relate to the struggle that is modern dating. It's been heart-wrenching, distressing, infuriating, annoying, terrifying, soul-crushing, and unsuitable for those with peanut allergies. And now, it's good content. Because it's been funny, too.

Some Terms
I WISH
I DIDN'T
KNOW

If you don't know the following terms, you're lucky, because a lot of them are somewhat bad things I hope have not happened to you. That being said, you'll be seeing these terms throughout the book, so get used to them.

Breadcrumbing:

Sending someone the bare minimum number of texts needed to make them believe "things" are still "on."

DTR:

Define The Relationship—putting a label on a casual fling. Congrats—you're now officially dating. Cool.

The Friend Zone:

When someone cruelly curses you by telling you they want to be friends instead of have sex.

Ghosting:

Not responding to someone's texts. This isn't a great thing to do, but neither is running the water in the bathroom without actually washing your hands, and we all do that anyway. Right?

Honeymoon Phase:

The early part of a relationship when you still like your partner. Feel free to skip this and go straight to boredom and constant bickering, if that's more your style.

IRL:

In real life, which is to say, not on the internet (as though that's not also real life—or is it? Hard to tell.)

Meet-Cute:

Meeting someone in a cute way, so at least you have a good story to tell your friends before the relationship inevitably goes up in flames.

RT:

Retweet, aka share someone's tweet on your page, aka validate their existence at the expense of your own.

Settling:

This is basically the same as dating. Well, more specifically, it's when you end up with something you don't really want because it's easy.

Slide into the DMs:

This happens when you think it's weird to ask someone for their phone number IRL, so you decide it's more normal to find them online and respond to their Instagram story with an eggplant emoji. It is a particularly confusing message, as the story was about their attempts to make their own baba ghanoush (so presumably they should have enough eggplant of their own).

Subtweet:

Talking shit about someone on Twitter without saying their name. It sounds mean, but it's often the only way to reach people.

Swiping:

The way to sort through profiles on a dating app, otherwise known as plyo-metrics for your thumb.

DATING Apps AND MEETING THE

RIGHT PERSON

I can only imagine the myth of Sisyphus was about dating apps. Hinge's motto might as well be, "Ten swipes a day, every single day, for the rest of your life." Dating apps are marketed as a way to make dating easier, but they're really just a way to make getting a *first* date easier. After that, you're still yourself, and everyone else is still themselves, and if you meet someone cute who has a cat you're allergic to, it's probably over. Besides, as with exercise and microwavable mac 'n' cheese, "easier" isn't always best. I often find myself giving my time to people I don't connect with at all simply because chatting with someone on Bumble was "easy."

One massive problem with dating apps is their popularity. We can now volume-date in a way we never could before. There are so many people on OkCupid that your perfect match might *always* be exactly one swipe away. They're probably not. But they could be. But they're not. And so you stay on Tinder forever. And you've accumulated eighty-nine dick pics. And you're miserable. And you start to wonder if you should cut out dating apps as the middleman and instead just start crying for no reason. But you never do. And that's the joy of online dating.

Mutually Scorned—A Proposal

Objective: Mutually Scorned is a dating app that seeks to match people who have rejected each other. Our research suggests that nothing gets a single person more interested than knowing someone doesn't like them back.

Product Description: A user builds a profile for Mutually Scorned the same way they do for most existing dating apps. They select their four best photos taken within a "reasonable time frame," determined by the user, and upload them to the app. The user can also choose to write a bio, which we highly encourage. The longer and more emoji-dense a bio is, the more likely a user is to be rejected and therefore get more matches.

Once a user's profile is complete, they begin looking at others' profiles. If they like someone, they swipe yes, and if they don't like someone or are in a particularly pissy mood, they swipe no. If two users swipe no on each other, a fun screen will pop up that says, "You think you're better than me!?" The two will be informed that neither thought the other was attractive, and they will be matched. Hooray!

We believe this chat screen will provide ample material for their early conversations. Maybe they thought they were too good for the other person initially, but once we inform them that they are, in fact, *not*, they'll likely hit it off.

Market Size: Who's using the app? Our in-house experts have predicted that we can reach most of the market made up of young adults who weren't hugged a satisfactory amount as children. We also believe we can corner the market on people who *were* hugged an acceptable amount but whose mothers regularly ask, "Why are you still single?" We also believe that in the future, we may be able to appeal to those who *were* hugged a satisfactory amount and *aren't* questioned regularly about their love lives—scientifically referred to as "defects"—if we emphasize the challenge of appealing to someone who lacked initial interest.

Competitors: Mutually Scorned does compete with traditional dating apps—Tinder, OkCupid, Hinge, Instagram. However its main competition consists of products that capitalize on human insecurity, such as those produced by wellness companies like Goop. People are only willing to put so many of their dollars toward alleviating their baseless insecurities, and we intend to fight $37 collagen-enhanced, antiaging, metabolism-revving green juice to the end for it. Mutually Scorned also competes against Reddit.com —the internet's foremost destination for finding people who don't like you.

Unique Edge: Mutually Scorned benefits from a user's desire to compete with themselves. When they realize how many people are rejecting them, they may become more invested in continuing to swipe in the hopes that perhaps, eventually, they'll stop racking up tons of matches. We will regularly send messages like, "You think you're too good for someone who doesn't even like you? That's dumb, and so are you," so the user is incentivized to lower their standards and go on more dates. This leads to happiness, we assume. Think about it.

Additionally, many users of traditional dating apps will swipe yes on profiles that don't interest them in order to get more matches. This helps them feel good about themselves, but it doesn't lead to serious dating. We avoid this pitfall altogether— nothing about Mutually Scorned will ever make a user feel good about themselves. Our users are there for serious dating—and serious rejection.

Celebrity Endorsements: Freud, we think, but he hasn't given a direct quote.

Potential Roadblocks: Users may begin to game the app. For example, a user might realize that if they want to be matched with someone, they have to swipe no on them, which means people are getting matched with people who actually find them attractive, which does mess everything up. Additionally to consider: People may use the app only to seek out their exes in an attempt to find out if they're still single, and then swipe no on them to feel powerful, and then end up matching with them. This messes everything up, but there's really nothing that can be done about that—it happens on every dating app. Finally, we have had users in our focus group describe the app as "hurtful." This may be something to revisit. Although, we do find Mutually Scorned no less offensive than the very existence of Tinder, so revisions to the framework are unlikely.

Management Team: Everyone on our management team is single, and most of our research into the efficacy of this product comes from existing in the world. We bring to the table years of experience in being turned on by rejection. We have not stopped to consider that the two phenomena may be connected, nor will we ever.

Ethical Considerations: None.

Mutually Scorned: Because Nothing Is Hotter Than Rejection.

How I Used Tinder Smart Photos to Prove Once and for All That I'm More Attractive than a Plate of Cold Refried Beans

This has been a rough year for me—I hit the wrong side of twenty-five, I got dumped, and my turtle ran away. I mean, I watched it go, but still. I didn't think I'd be able to turn things around, but then I realized something. Maybe I could get some of my confidence back if only I answered the age-old question: Am I more attractive than a plate of cold refried beans? Of course, the answer to that question would unlock everything! And maybe Tinder was the key.

Tinder "smart photos" is a feature that uses an algorithm to determine which of your photos is most successful for getting you matches and the classy "DTF" messages (stands for "Down to Fuck," often confused with "Don't Try Franzia"—a classic piece of wisdom). Tinder then automatically shows that photo first when people are swiping on your profile. To conduct this experiment and find out whether or not I really am more attractive than a plate of cold refried beans, I needed a set of test data—five of my best photos.

There was a catch. If I made just one Tinder account with five pictures of me and one plate of cold refried beans, the best one might be a picture of me followed by the plate of cold refried beans followed by four more pictures of me. If this happened, I'd only find out which picture was the best, not the full ranking of the remaining four pictures—I could beat the plate of cold refried beans at my sister's wedding, but not in general. Therefore, to conclude *definitively* that I'm more attractive all around than a plate of cold refried beans, I needed to make five separate Tinder accounts. On each account, I'd upload two photos: one of me, and one of a plate of cold refried beans.

For consistency, I used the same picture of a plate of cold refried beans every time. How'd I get this picture, you might ask? I fried beans. Then I fried them again. Then I left them out overnight. Because I'm a goddamn scientist.

My test pictures were the following:

1. Me from a very high angle to accentuate my best feature, namely my knowledge of which photo angle makes me look skinny.

2. Me doing stand-up comedy to demonstrate my wit and charm though probably just my wit.

3. Me and my sister to show how family-oriented I am, and also to trick people into thinking I'm twenty-one.

4. Me in a Safeway parking lot to demonstrate my love for the great outdoors.

5. Me in a bikini because, as my mother used to say: "If you don't have a bikini pic on Tinder, you're probably less sexy than a plate of cold refried beans."

6. A plate of cold refried beans.

I was now ready to begin Tinder-ing. I wanted to make sure the experiment had time to collect an adequate amount of data, so I left each account open for a day, logged which picture won, deleted the Tinder account, and then made a new one. For keeping track of data of this magnitude, I'd recommend an SQL server, a MongoDB database, or an Excel spreadsheet, or you could write the results in eyeliner on your inner thigh. I chose the eyeliner because I wanted to be able to iterate quickly, but please offer feedback if you think there are other ways I could improve upon the data collection portion of the experiment.

After the first four days of my experiment, the score was GINNY: 4; PLATE OF COLD REFRIED BEANS: 0. Things were looking good for this girl—it was like my turtle had come back to roost. I just had to get through one more photo—the dreaded bikini pic. I'm always nervous about my swimsuit bod, perhaps owing to my affinity for eating cold refried beans for dinner, but science doesn't stop for insecurities. At least, I don't think it does. I'm not actually a goddamn scientist.

I braced myself for a challenging day ahead as I made a new Tinder profile that was just my body and the beans. Around 9 p.m., I was still too scared to look at the results. What would I find? Could my self-esteem handle the knowledge that people would rather bang a fart-inducing, shit-like substance than my naked body? That refried beans, the peanut butter of legumes,* were more enticing than me, a real-life human woman? I was about to find out.

At midnight, I was ready to see the final results. I held my breath as the app loaded. What would it be?! Me? Or the legumes? It stalled—damn my slow Wi-Fi. It stalled again, but that's because I dramatically threw my phone into a pillow. Then I had to pause again because I realized I hadn't checked Twitter in twenty-nine seconds. After seeing no new tweets and scrolling through #babiesresemblingdannydevito instead for twenty minutes, I returned to Tinder, on the edge of my seat. And then I saw it. *It was my bikini pic!*

I AM MORE BEAUTIFUL THAN A PLATE OF COLD REFRIED BEANS! WHAT A TIME TO BE ALIVE!

I've obviously been on cloud nine since the conclusion of this experiment. If I were to extend my analysis, I'd want to know if I'm sexier than other plates of cold food, such as plates of cold spaghetti or plates of cold broccoli, but there's only so much I can do at once. I'd also want to see how I compare with stuff like grass and pavement. But for now, I'm just happy knowing I'm more attractive than a plate of cold refried beans. Truly a wonderful day.

(originally seen on mcsweeneys.net)

*Apparently peanuts *are* legumes. Like I said, I'm not actually a goddamn scientist.

Automatic Out-of-Office Replies for Dating Apps

○ ○ ○   Subject: ○○○

Thank you for your Tinder message. I will be unable to respond to any dick pics until I've completed eight more hours of therapy. For immediate assistance, please try your own therapist.

○ ○ ○   Subject: ○○○

Apologies for missing your message. If you're writing to say that my tits look good in picture 2, please direct compliments to Sarah, the sales clerk at Victoria's Secret. If you're writing to ask if I'd like to get a drink, please ask for my number and then text me promptly but not too promptly, if you think you're someone I'd be interested in (not you, Steve). If you're writing to ask if my little sister from picture 3 is single, please rethink who you are as a person.

○ ○ ○   Subject: ○○○

I will be off Hinge from the onset of my PMS symptoms (August 2) until the conclusion of my menstrual cycle (August 18 of the following year). I will not respond to your message upon my return, as you called me "baybe," which is neither the correct spelling of "babe" nor "baby," both of which are inappropriate for an opening message.

○ ○ ○   Subject: ○○○

Taking a 30-day break following being asked for photos of my feet— please try again at the end of the month.

Regards,

The Whole Team (me and both feet— Ren and Stimpy)

I am unable to take your message at this time. If this is an emergency, please hang up and use a different service. This is a dating app.

I am actively using this dating app, but I will not be responding to you.

Working on a new project for the next three weeks—dating/fixing a 37-year-old DJ who considers texting while driving an "art"—and will not be responding as quickly as usual. For a faster response, try me on LinkedIn or use proper grammar.

I've received your message. Please circle back when you're ready for something serious and also have done a complete overhaul on your personality. At that point, we can get the ball rolling, hit the ground running, think outside the box, action the project, dot the i's and cross the t's, and add some value to this results-driven game plan. If you're cute.

Entering an area with limited Wi-Fi (my apartment, after I turned the Wi-Fi off in frustration at the content of my incoming Bumble messages). Will do my best to respond by Monday. Don't hold your breath, as my response will likely be no, particularly if the question is, "wassup qt?"

I am not reading messages right now, but I will respond to you ASAP (After Squandering All-other Prospects).

Thank you for swiping right. Your Bumble match is important to me, as my self-esteem depends on it. I will not be able to get back to you within the next 24 hours because letting the match expire is the best-case scenario for this interaction.

What's the Right Dating App for You to Settle Down with?

Your chosen dating app may well be the longest relationship of your adult life. And there aren't enough to choose from—they should make one for people who are actually cool. Plus, they're dangerous—you could get murdered, or worse, stuck in a four-hour-long, one-sided conversation with some dude named Dave (it's interesting that "manslaughter" and "man's laughter" are spelled the same). But we have the dating apps we have, so we might as well try to find the best one. Determining which app is the ideal match for you to strike out with for all of eternity can be tricky, so take our quiz to find your match.

1. What's your ideal Friday night?

a. Dinner and a movie with someone

b. Sex with someone and a movie by myself

c. Internet-stalking my ex in great detail, which is often the healthier alternative to reading the news

d. Discussing philosophers I haven't read but still definitely know a ton about

e. Sitting astern while the captain goes aft

2. What adjective best describes you?

a. Normal

b. Loose

c. Curious, in the way that killed the cat

d. Socially awkward, which is to say, very smart

e. Wet

3. What type of car do you drive?

a. A Toyota

b. A motorcycle

c. A self-driving Tesla. What I know, my car knows.

d. You know when you get to a parking lot, and you're like, "Damn, whose car is that?" That's my car. And not just because there's a small baby lion in a cage strapped to the top of it.

e. A dinghy—the Car of the Sea

4. What's your favorite food?

a. What's the cool new Thai place in Silver Lake? I like what everyone else likes.

b. Tabasco sauce

c. Soylent

d. Foie gras and my own opinions

e. Fresh seaweed

5. What quality most attracts you to someone else?

a. Easy to talk to

b. Looks

c. I need to process six thousand petabytes of information on any individual person before I can even begin to think about crunching the numbers on whether or not we'd have even the tiniest semblance of compatibility.

d. Academic prestige, duh. It doesn't *have* to be Harvard, but it should be.

e. Fins

6. What are you looking for in a failed relationship?

a. Commitment

b. One (1) instance of casual sex

c. For all of my browsing data to get sold to nefarious private entities

d. A person to be impressed with my thick book. I didn't write it, but I'm about to consider starting to read it. And it's *thick*. Like, *thicc*.

e. A companion to warm the starboard with me

7. What's your favorite sex position?

a. Missionary

b. Doing sex

c. Doggie style, so I can check my phone

d. The valedictorian (If this isn't a real position, I will invent it.)

e. The waterfall; I am always wet (*nice*)

8. What do you do for work?

a. Marketing

b. A million and a half freelance gigs that I'll intentionally try to hide from you. I don't want people up in my business.

c. Engineering at Generic Massive Tech Company™

d. Um, I'm a consultant at Consulting Company. Surely you've heard of it. No, I will not explain what I do.

e. I fish.

9. Do you know the exact longitudinal coordinates of the Trobriand Islands?

a. No, but I can tell you right now how much a flight to Cabo costs.

b. No, and it's irrelevant. I'd never go on vacation with a partner.

c. No, but I can figure it out.

d. No, I don't think so, unless—wait—is that where Fyre Festival was? In that case, I've been.

e. Yes.

Results:

....

All a's: Hinge. Congratulations—you like what everyone likes. Go on Hinge to find the widest array of lackluster options.

All b's: Tinder. You can't be tamed, and by tamed I mean pressured into a relationship with the tiniest modicum of commitment. Go on Tinder to stay "free" forever, whatever that means.

All c's: Facebook Dating. You need every single solitary piece of information about someone before you're willing to settle down with them, and that's convenient, because you have it. Backed by Facebook, your data supply is *ripe*.

All d's: The League. You went to a fancy college and want everyone to know. The League is like the the dating app equivalent of wearing a Harvard sweatshirt to an engagement party—you were barely invited, so don't eat all the shrimp.

All e's: Sea Captain Date. It's time to set sail.

A combination: Download every dating app. You're inconsistent, and you're going to need to blanket your phone with matches to find literally anyone.

Dating App Questionnaires That Reflect What I'd Actually Want to Know About a Potential Partner

I'm going to let out a bloodcurdling scream the next time a dating app asks me if I prefer hamsters to mice (mice—duh. Who among us hasn't been traumatized by losing the third-grade class hamster?). I've gone on approximately "too many" terrible first dates, and it's because dating apps aren't asking the right questions to filter for the type of people I'd *actually* want to go out with. Here are some recommendations for more relevant Qs.

- Can we watch all of *Love Island* in a row? British and American?

- Can you name all five Spice Girls? No Googling.

- Sports? Do you do or watch them? More importantly, will you ever make me?

- What's your stance on doing dishes?

- What's your stance on respecting people? Pro, con, or libertarian?

- Do you regularly interrupt people in convers—

- Do you still watch your ex's Instagram stories?

- Will you still watch my Instagram stories?

- Within an hour of me posting them?

- Maybe forty-five minutes?

- Will you hug my mom? But not in a weird way, okay? You know what I mean. Some people hug moms a little *too* tightly.

- Do you want *my* kids? (I don't know why Hinge doesn't specify this.)

- Are you a bot? And I don't mean like a computer program, I mean like do you have emotional intelligence?

- Is it okay if I'm in a bad mood 70 percent of the time?

- 80 percent?

- 90 percent?

- 95 percent?

- What color are your bedsheets? This is just to confirm you have them. Also, I sometimes like to match my outfit to them, so please try to have them not be orange.

- Have you ghosted anyone in the past forty-eight months?

- Are you open to committing to a relationship in the next five to seven years?

- Do you use the term "tied down" to describe the experience of being in a stable relationship with a loving partner?

- Are you kind?

- Oh, sorry, I didn't finish typing the last one. Are you kind of a dick?

A Match Made in Heaven

God swiveled around in Her chair. It would have been plenty easy to get swivel chairs for everyone else involved in the project, too, but God needed to assert Herself. You didn't make it on "30 Under 30" by handing out swivel chairs.

"I don't want to keep rolling the dice with the One Percent's mutual funds—they're the last humans I'd want to screw over—but I do need to make a big, profound move. I'm tired of being snubbed from this list. Even the founders of Lyft were on it. I'm thinking it's time I start a company that matters."

"Well, God, you could always check out the finance side instead. Nowhere in the Bible does it say you have to build the apps yourself. Have you tried angel investing?"

The entire room turned to face Chad and Babs, the angels. "We just do PR," Chad said quickly. "We don't ask where the funding comes from."

"Of course *you* wouldn't," said Babs, saltily.

"Here, Babs? You're really going to do this *here*? At *work*? Sorry I started dating humans, but you can still make an effort to keep things professional," Chad responded.

"Wait, you're *dating* humans?" God asked. "Why are humans interested in *you*?"

"Great question," said Babs. "My thoughts exactly. I suspect they only like him because he lies about being five foot ten on Hinge."

"Wait, back up—humans still care about that?" God asked. She was bewildered—screw the meeting; this was news. These venture capitalists she'd pulled up from Earth were dull, anyway. She usually didn't let finance people into Heaven—not because of anything they'd done, they're just boring as Hell. "I gave them stepladders because the height thing was getting in the way of them finding their Soul Mate."

"Oh, no, people don't believe in the Soul Mate thing anymore," said Chad. "Thank God."

"You're welcome," God said. "But I'm still confused. If people aren't using dating apps to find their Soul Mates, what are they even looking for? What criteria are they using to judge their matches?"

"You know, the basics. Age, where they went to college, height, if their opening message includes a misspelling, jawlines, vague vibe," said Chad. "I thought the whole Soul Mates thing was a myth."

"Jawlines? *Jawlines?* People are pairing off based on *jawlines?*" God was clearly behind on this season's *CW* offerings.

"Sure, I mean, if you're making a decision based on a few photos, not everyone has access to a cute dog. What's wrong with jawlines?"

"What's wrong with jawlines?!" God was flabbergasted. "Humans are the most complex creatures I created—I gave them emotions and anxiety disorders and brains that can barely fit through their mothers' . . . you know . . . on the way out. I gave them music and math and advanced physics and upward of nine Taylor Swift albums. But I didn't do this all for fun—"

"Why *are* the brains too big to fit? Some of the ladies in my book club wanted to know—" Babs started.

"It's so that one day, someday, each human would sift through the billions on the planet and find the person, or people, whose myriad quirks most intricately and most perfectly interlock with their own. I gave every stupid, complex being a Soul Mate! Those with whom they fit perfectly *in their souls*! Those who help them unlock the key to a satisfying life!"

"Well then what's the point of dating apps at all?" Chad asked.

"I just assumed they could be like a subscription service to get people to their Soul Mate faster! But you're telling me they pair off based on nothing but *jawlines*? I only threw those in at the last minute because I wanted them to enjoy crunchy peanut butter. I'm a benevolent God!"

"Um, it's not just jawlines, there's also height—"

"Again, with the height!" God bellowed. "That's even worse! Randy was five foot four and he gave me six orgasms in a row."

"Through just intercourse?" Babs asked. It was inappropriate, but she wanted to know.

"No, of course not. Don't be ridiculous," snapped God.

Babs hung her head. She'd hoped perhaps a female deity might cum vaginally, but no, that was still asking too much.

"Alright." God took a deep breath. "I think we've found our answer. Let's all look at this as an opportunity. We'll build a dating app. One that works. One that shows people their Soul Mate. I hadn't realized what a disaster everything must be down there on Earth. No wonder the humans invented cauliflower rice—they're miserable. But I'll fix it. I'll give everyone their Soul Mate, they can all find eternal bliss, and the app will go completely viral. And then, I'll get on '30 Under 30'—just like Randy did."

"I know a *lot* about love," said Chad at their first official planning meeting the next day.

"I beg to differ," said Babs. "When we were dating, you got me a Fitbit for Christmas. Do you have any idea how offensive—"

"Okay, okay, let's stay on track," said God. "On the one hand, making this app should be easy. We're giving people their perfect match—the person I explicitly put on Earth to fill all of their voids—don't giggle, Chad, you're a child—to validate their existence. Once they actually *use* it, they'll be eternally happy, so that's nice. On the other hand, though, they might not be willing to download it at all. I say we give it to them at a discount first, and then immediately jack up the price." Having a female God didn't change Her profit motive, it turned out.

Babs and Chad had their doubts. Whether or not a dating app gave people good matches had no effect on how popular it was. No, a dating app was popular for one reason and one reason only—if users felt *cool* being on it. If it was exclusive. If all the men were cool and attractive. Like Raya, but if all the men were cool and attractive. But everyone had a soul—there was nothing elite about God's idea. However, She was resolute.

"Humans should trust me," She said. "I'm God—I've never caused any problems."

And so, within a few days, they had created V1 of Soul Mates—like Postmates, but for Souls (it was God's name, not theirs). Chad liked the name Datyng! (the exclamation mark was silent) and Babs preferred Quizzinc__ (the underscores were not silent).

The product was fairly simple. Unlike traditional dating apps, there was no swiping through potential matches. The user just had to log into their Google account so God could access their search history, the easiest way to identify a being's one true character. That way, God could find your exact Soul Mate and show you one profile. You'd then be given their Instagram handle and could DM them. In V2, God might consider humans who don't have Instagrams, but She couldn't deal with fringe cases just yet.

All that was left to do was test it on a group of real-life humans. God picked eighteen of them—eight sets of Soul Mates, with some sets being made up of more than two people. She called them up to Heaven to match them off. Once they realized the people they got paired up with were their *true* Soul Mates—the ones they were meant to be with forever, the ones to bring them eternal personal satisfaction, the ones to make them finally "get" Wes Anderson movies—they'd surely tell their friends to download the app. And once Soul Mates had gone viral, the silly time-suck that was modern dating would be null. People would just be happy. And, more importantly, God would finally get that highly coveted spot on "30 Under 30." The spot that would make Randy jealous. At last.

Unfortunately, the focus group didn't go as planned.

"Am I dead?" asked Sandra, a lawyer from Houston. "Because if so, I need to arrange for someone to feed my cat."

"Is this jury duty?" asked Nadya, a PhD student from Rhode Island. "I'm not a U.S. citizen, I shouldn't have to."

"When's lunch?" Derek, a Canadian jockey, wanted to know. "This seems like the kind of thing that should have croissants, at least."

He was right. They were in a conference room. Croissants *should* have been there.

"Welcome, everyone," said Babs. "You're not serving jury duty; there are no croissants; and, no, you're not dead. You're part of a focus group for a new dating app, Soul Mates, that matches you with your Soul Mates. You'll only be here a few hours, and then you can go back down to Earth and spend a joyful eternity with them." She looked at her watch. "Ideally, you can even have dinner down there. We didn't budget for takeout."

"Ugh, no," said Sandra. "No no no no no. I quit dating months ago. I promised my therapist."

"But you consented to the focus group—"

"Only for the Olive Garden gift card, I didn't read what it was about. I don't date, let me out of here."

"It's not dating," said Chad. "We're just going to give you your Soul Mate. You don't have to do any sifting or scouting or judging or waxing or primping or anything else you do when you date—"

"Do you do those things?" Babs asked. "It sure didn't seem like—"

"We're going to assign you a partner or partners, and they're your perfect match. You'll be completely settled," said Chad.

"How do we know they're our perfect match?"

"Do we split the bill? Because I don't want to."

"Are we on a reality TV show?"

"Can we have sex?"

"STOP YELLING!" Chad screamed. "You have to ask your questions one at a time." He pointed to a short man with an obvious toupee.

"I'm already married," said Frank.

Babs and Chad exchanged a nervous look. Was there a mistake? The angels didn't pride themselves on being particularly angelic, but they didn't want to be home-wreckers, either.

"But not to your Soul Mate," God said, speaking for the first time. No one had noticed She was there. "And that's why you're here."

Frank looked relieved. Maybe he didn't think his wife was his Soul Mate, either.

"I'm God, and I'll be the one in charge of this focus group from now on. It seems you're all a little mixed up, and I understand why. Humans have been messing up dating for millennia, and if I'd known, I'd have stepped in earlier. There are actually a lot of problems on Earth that I don't really know much about, so I'd prefer people stop cursing my name, but that's neither here nor there. The point is, today, for the first time ever, you get to go on a date with the person I picked out for you—the one person you were destined to be with. The one person who will finally make you feel *whole*."

"But I don't need a partner to feel whole," said Ty, a nurse from Romania. "I'm happy on my own, I don't need to be completed."

"Yes, you do," said God. "You're unfinished. That's how I made you."

"For a Lady God, you sure do sound like the patriarchy—"

"Let me explain," said God. "Do you all know that feeling when you're in a relationship, and you think it would be somewhat convenient if your ears just magically burned off, because you can't bear to hear their laugh one more time, as it reminds you of a llama taking a shit?"

Everyone nodded. Everyone knew that feeling.

"Do you all know that feeling when your partner walks into a room, and you feel like a SWAT team has just taken up residence inside your lungs, because that's how invasive you find their very presence?"

Everyone nodded. Everyone knew that feeling.

"Do you all know that feeling when you're annoyed that your partner bought you flowers? Because even though it's a kind gesture, everything they do must be to deliberately annoy you?"

Everyone nodded. Everyone knew that feeling. Except Frank—no one had ever bought him flowers.

"And when you're alone, do you know that feeling, scrolling through the Criterion Channel and wondering if anyone will ever love you, because it feels like no one ever has? And wondering if it has something to do with your passion for the Criterion Channel? And then you think *maybe* your therapist loves you, because she shows you so much kindness, but then you remember you pay her, and you bury your head in your pillow while a reality show that depicts the worst people in the world finding love plays on in the background? And you wonder—why them, but not me?"

Everyone nodded. Everyone knew that feeling.

"That's because the people you're with aren't your Soul Mates," said God. "Maybe you're attracted to them, and maybe they have a perfectly symmetrical face, and maybe they make a ton of money. A shit ton of money—I do let some of you make a *lot* of money. But that's not what matters if they're not your Soul Mate. Your Soul Mates are the only people on the whole planet whom you can actually exist beside, for all of eternity, without ever even *wondering* why you were born a human, not a frog. They're the people who don't annoy you—not even when you're PMS-ing, if you're one of the unlucky ones I cursed with that condition. Because you were meant to be with them. They're your *Soul Mate.*"

The humans looked skeptical.

"But if Soul Mates could be anyone regardless of what they look like and how successful they are, why do celebrities always date other celebrities?"

"Because celebrities are better than regular people, so they obviously only work with each other. Think of it like a sort of ranking, soul-wise. Your Soul Mate is your equivalent."

The humans nodded. This made sense. Celebrities were better than regular people.

"So, assuming you're all on board, when I call your name, come to the front to get matched with your Soul Mate, or Soul Mates. There's a chariot waiting for you outside to enjoy your first date together. You'll return back here in four hours to discuss your experience with the group, so we can iterate on the app, should changes be needed. And then we'll send you back down to Earth, where you can tell all your friends about how wonderfully it worked. Oh, and your chariot will include a six-pack of Sprite, from our official sponsor."

Everyone calmed down. They were still skeptical, but the complimentary Sprite seemed to mollify them. Enough to try, at least.

"By the way," said God, as they made their way out. "Of course you can have sex in Heaven. Please be fruitful about it."

While the Soul Mating was happening, God looked Randy up on LinkedIn. She knew she shouldn't, but it was so tempting. Damn it, She thought. After being named on "30 Under 30," he seemed to have gotten a massive round of Series C funding for his start-up—environmentally friendly backpacks for kids. God was pissed. You can't just dump me and then become successful, She said to Herself. God snapped Her fingers in a fit of jealous rage and halted global warming—anything to run Randy's company into the ground.

Four hours later, the humans returned. For a group of people who'd just spent an afternoon with their perfect matches, they looked generally quite miserable. Frank alone seemed to be beaming. He had his arm around Sandra, who most certainly did *not* want it there.

"Welcome back, lovers! Did everyone have a good experience?" asked God.

Most people shook their heads no. She was confused—they were acting the way She did after a bad first date. Defeated, miserable, pessimistic. This isn't how someone should act when they'd just met their Soul Mate.

"What's wrong?" God asked.

"She doesn't like baseball," said Trina. "That's sort of a deal-breaker for me."

God looked to Patsy, her match. "No, no. You're a perfect match, in your souls. This is about your serious, real matches. It's not about who you can watch a game with. It's about who will eliminate that nagging feeling of emptiness that plagues your every moment, the one that's always with you."

"I don't have that feeling," said Trina.

"Yes, you do," said God.

Trina thought for a moment. "Oh, wait, you're right, now that I'm paying attention, I feel it," said Trina. "But I can't with Patsy. I watch baseball every Saturday, it's a deal-breaker for me."

They weren't the only dissenters.

"Nadya used the phrase 'Happy Monday,'" said Derek. "That just doesn't work for me. There's nothing happy about Mondays."

"That's just a phrase, that's not a measure of compatibility," said God. She was beginning to understand why they were all single, except Frank. They were annoying. Frank was also annoying, just not single.

"Okay, well, maybe you two should just exchange numbers and get back in touch later," Babs suggested, trying to be helpful. She knew what the humans were upset about, but she wanted to impress God.

"Yeah, when you realize what an idiotic excuse that is," said God. "Anyone else?"

"His socks didn't match."

"So get new socks," said God.

"She misspelled 'weather.'"

"How would you even know, it was in person," God tried to rebut.

"He took a phone call from his mom mid-makeout."

"She doesn't like Dave Matthews Band."

"She likes the Dixie Chicks."

"He voted for Mitt Romney."

"She insisted on oat milk."

"You should have warned me first that my soul is attracted to much older people."

"She lives in Milwaukee."

"He chewed a pungent, fruity gum."

"I don't date coworkers."

"He's a Taurus, and ugly."

"He's not Timothée Chalamet."

"She's not my ex. No one will ever be my ex."

"They're annoying."

"He is my ex. Why'd you do this to me?"

"We just didn't vibe."

God was at a loss. She looked helplessly to Chad and Babs. The complaints were endless. They hadn't been persuaded by Her benevolent mission. She felt ignored. She'd given every single human in the study their perfect matches, and it seemed like not *one* was grateful. She looked to Frank and Sandra. While everyone in the group had a Soul Mate, Frank and Sandra were the *most* perfect together. A rare Super-Soul-Mate—the kind that was so perfect for each other, they could hygienically share a toothbrush, because even their plaque was a perfect match.

"I hated him," said Sandra. Frank's smile dissolved. "We aren't meant to be."

"Yes, you are," said God. "I've looked across every metric that matters—how you treat others, what you value, how good of a human you are, your kindness, your empathy. Frank is a perfect match. A *particularly* perfect match. What could possibly be the issue?"

Frank was embarrassed. He wished this conversation could take place in a separate room, but it was useful feedback. Frank's marriage was falling apart. Maybe he'd benefit from knowing what women thought of him.

"Those things just don't matter to me," said Sandra. "They're not the most important."

"Having an identical soul? Knowing you're so compatible you'll never grow apart? Knowing you'll be just a little bit empty forever without them? That doesn't matter to you?" God was about to explode, and the results of that were *never* good.

"Okay, well, the problem was . . . " Sandra stalled. She felt guilty saying it, but it had to be said. She looked over at Frank. Looked *down* at Frank, more accurately. "He's only five foot seven."

The other humans nodded sympathetically. They understood immediately why the pair would never work out. Frank *was* only five foot seven.

"That's absurd," said God, flummoxed. Height *again*? Was She really going to have to remind them that Randy made her cum *six times in a row,* at all of five feet four inches? "Did anyone else take issue with their Soul Mate's height?" she asked.

A number of others nodded. God was pissed. The experiment seemed to have failed.

"Does this height obsession make sense to you?" God asked Babs and Chad.

"Yes," said Babs.

"No," said Chad. Chad was five foot six.

Unable to calm the participants, God sent them back down to Earth. She'd really thought She was onto something with Soul Mates, but maybe not. Maybe She didn't understand people as well as She thought She did. And maybe that's why She was alone, missing Randy, without even the possibility of getting his attention with "30 Under 30" since the loser humans weren't even going to recommend Soul Mates to their friends.

God picked up Her phone and opened up Soul Mates, logging into Her own account. She hadn't ever tried it before. God was pretty quick to give humans a product She'd never tested, because She *knew* Her Soul Mate was Randy, and She'd figured getting matched with him would probably just make Her sad.

But She was feeling curious. The app loaded and—*Frank?* No, that can't be right. Short was one thing, but Frank was . . . short *and* Frank. Like, choose one.

God closed Soul Mates and opened Hinge instead. Her first match was a corporate lawyer named Wayne who seemed to have a very expensive car.

Just looking for someone to talk about existentialism with. 5'9"

God swiped right, hoping for the best.

No way you're under 30, Wayne wrote back, three weeks later.

No way you're under 30

Ignore Dating App Red Flags

It baffles me when people actually use red flags as a reason not to start dating someone. In my experience, red flags have one purpose and one purpose only—something to cite after the relationship goes down in flames as proof that you knew all along it wasn't right. If you notice some red flags on the dating apps and want to follow my reasoning for how to ignore them, read on.

They say, "I'm not looking for anything serious" in their bio.

HOW TO IGNORE IT: You'll change them. You're into DIY.

Their profile says they're 42,908,422 miles away, but they invited you to their apartment.

HOW TO IGNORE IT: You love to travel.

They ask if you want to see a picture of their dick.

HOW TO IGNORE IT: At least they asked!

They list their interests as "sex" and "oral sex."

HOW TO IGNORE IT: There's something alluring about specificity.

Pictures of them holding knives.

HOW TO IGNORE IT: A chef! How nice the foie gras will be.

Their opening message includes a reference to your tits.

HOW TO IGNORE IT: Maybe they meant to say, "Nice zits." Actually, that's a redder flag.

They ask again if you want to see a picture of their dick.

HOW TO IGNORE IT: So few guys ask follow-up questions. At least he's paying attention to the conversation!

No face pictures.

HOW TO IGNORE IT: You like the mystique.

No pictures at all.

HOW TO IGNORE IT: Even more mystique.

Their profile disappears from the app two days after you match, but they keep texting you. Did they delete it? Were they forced off?

HOW TO IGNORE IT: Maybe it's just a bug on the site. Or maybe they just already decided you're in a relationship! That's sweet—there are too many players out there.

You Google them and learn they're still legally married to someone else.

HOW TO IGNORE IT: Who cares about laws? Do you know what else is a law—the Second Amendment.

They ask for your Venmo.

HOW TO IGNORE IT: They're a feminist and want to split the bill.

You receive 14 emails from Instagram saying someone is trying to log into your account.

HOW TO IGNORE IT: Notifications give you a dopamine rush.

They ask for your Social Security number.

HOW TO IGNORE IT: They're taking an interest in your life! Maybe they've decided you're in it for the long haul, and these are the sorts of things they'll have to know in case you're ever in a motorcycle accident. No, you don't own a motorcycle *per se*, but still.

You can no longer log onto your online banking account.

HOW TO IGNORE IT: You were spending too much money, anyway.

An FBI agent just showed up at your house.

HOW TO IGNORE IT: Maybe *he's* single.

Apparently, your net worth was wiped out.

HOW TO IGNORE IT: Let's be real—it wasn't that much.

The CIA has suggested you move.

HOW TO IGNORE IT: You wanted to improve your relationship with your parents anyway, and now you get to move back in with them.

You have to build a whole new life.

HOW TO IGNORE IT: This is your chance to finally go blonde. There's never been a more perfect opportunity.

Their profile says "Live Laugh Love" on it.

HOW TO IGNORE IT: It's impossible to dismiss this one. Swipe left.

Characters from Classic Rom-Coms Match on Tinder

When Harry Met Sally

May 3rd, 1989, 2:05 p.m.

Sally: If this doesn't work out at least we can be friends

Harry: hmm idk

Sally: I've met all my best guy friends on Tinder

Harry: rly?

Sally: Sort of. I've matched with guys I'm friends with IRL and messaged them, "LOL this is so funny."

Harry: it's not that funny

Sally: It is if you're friends.

Harry: those guys all wanted to sleep with you

Sally: Lol no they just wanted to friendly-cuddle! And occasionally have friendly sex.

March 12, 1995, 3:02 a.m.

Harry: u up?

Sally: You're right, I love you

Harry: lol cool wanna come over?

How to Lose a Guy in Ten Days

Benjamin Barry: heyyyy. Funny bio lol. I like the part where you say "I'm cray!!!" 15 times.

Andie Anderson: I'm cray!!!

Benjamin Barry: hahaha tbh all women are cray

Andie Anderson: Ughhh I wanted it to be my thing

Andie Anderson: Cuckoo cuckoo cuckooooo that's me!!

Benjamin Barry: can we meet up tonight?

Andie Anderson: I live with my mom and grandma

Benjamin Barry: the more the merrier

Andie Anderson: I wear tutus to the gym

Benjamin Barry: hot

Andie Anderson: I've already looked up the addresses of all your ex-lovers

Benjamin Barry: quick on your feet, I like it

Andie Anderson: I'll do anything to be professionally successful

Benjamin Barry: ok that's actually too much, i'm out

She's All That

Zack: hey

Laney Boggs: are you making fun of me? I know you'd never go for me. I wear glasses.

Zack: take off your glasses one time

Laney Boggs: why

Zack: just try it. send a pic

Laney Boggs: you can't send pics on Tinder

Zack: ok here's my number, text it to me

Laney Boggs: ok

Zack: sweet. I'm a talent scout, we can sign you for Ford Models

Laney Boggs: but what about my paintings?

Zack: Laney. With your glasses on, you're objectively just a regular super hot girl. But with them off—you're a supermodel.

Laney Boggs: Ugh fine

Hitch

Hitch: Hey

Sara: You think your tricks will work on me???

Hitch: I don't want to rush into things

Sara: Is that one of your classic moves?

Hitch: Can I buy you dinner?

Sara: I bet you say that to every insanely beautiful woman you ask on a date

Hitch: I do, actually

Sara: Well it's not going to work on *me*

Hitch: Ok, fine. I'll just be honest and tell you I love you

Sara: love you too

Crazy Rich Asians

Nick: hey what's up

Rachel: my career! What about you?

Nick: Ugh my needy family. Want to meet them? They're in Singapore

Rachel: I guess, ya. Is there anything I need to know about them?

Nick: nah

Nick: they're average rich

Nick: maybe slightly above

Nick: "comfortable"

Nick: they own a few islands ok, and they'll never accept you

Nick: They'll intentionally try to make your life a living hell because you're not good enough, and there's nothing I will do to help. It will be like that movie *Carrie*, kinda.

Rachel: Oh, I meant like, their names

Jerry Maguire

Jerry: Hello

Dorothy: ya got me!

Her

Theodore: I think I'm in love with you

Her: I am the virtual assistant helping you set up your profile. You have not yet finished creating a Tinder account.

Notting Hill

William: i fricken can't anymore with these fake accounts. USE REAL PICS, YOU'RE NOT ANNA SCOTT!!!!

Anna Scott: I'm just a girl, standing in front of a boy, asking him to believe that that's really me. Some of us actually *are* Anna Scott.

William: I'm reporting this account

You've Got Mail

Joe: How's your day?

Kathleen: Not good! I work at a cute little bookstore called Borders, and Amazon is trying to put us out of business.

Joe: dam sry

Kathleen: They're evil! They're so evil! They don't care about books at all. They only care about delivering things in like 2 seconds and not paying workers!!

Joe: idk if they can actually do it in 2 seconds

Kathleen: what?

Joe: Can we talk about something else? Do you like miniature poodles?

Kathleen: Is Joe your real name?

Joe: uhhh

Kathleen: What's your last name?

Joe: uhhh

Kathleen: Send me your LinkedIn

(Joe sends a link.)

Kathleen: What?! You're actually Jeff Bezos?!

Love Actually

Billy Mack: Wait, Tinder allows group chats now?

13 Going on 30

Automated message: We've confirmed that as a 13-year-old, you are too young for this app. If you'd like to use it anyway, please lie about your age and create a new account to protect us from legal ramifications, like we know you were already going to.

Tell Friends You Met Your Partner in Real Life

You're in a new relationship, and that's great! There's just one problem—you met your partner in real life. We all know it's embarrassing to confess that the two of you didn't meet online. What kind of dinosaur are you? Alas, not everyone is charming enough or sufficiently good at selfies to be successful on Tinder—some people must rely on their physical presence as a last resort. If this is true of you and your partner, here are some helpful tips for telling friends and family the *real* story.

Explain that you weren't meeting anyone worthwhile online. It's a common misconception that women who meet people in real life are desperate. What, were you so incapable of finding a decent person on Coffee Meets Bagel that you had to resort to making eye contact with strangers like a freak? Look, if that's your humiliating situation, just make peace with it and blame it on your matches.

Be patient. Your friends are probably just confused and need a little help coming to terms with what you're trying to tell them. Explain the logistics of meeting in person. Sometimes someone will send you a drink at a bar, which is the equivalent of getting a notification. If they're still struggling, try slapping your partner's face a few times to demonstrate the real-life swiping process.

Provide examples of other couples that met in real life. There are a lot of IRL relationships that work out! Your grandparents, for example. Blake Lively and Ryan Reynolds, I think. Ross and Rachel (you may need to go fictional if you run out of options).

Use metaphors. Meeting in real life is like using Yahoo! instead of Google. Sure, it's outdated and no one does it. Actually, that's the whole metaphor. The point is, at least Yahoo! still *exists*.

Blame the Wi-Fi connection. It's Starbucks's fault you couldn't meet online.

Lie. These days, every wedding toast includes an adorable story of how the groom was about to quit Tinder when he saw a beautiful photo of the bride and her second cousin's golden retriever. You can have that, too—just make up an OkCupid meet-cute: *It was a rainy Sunday afternoon. You were scrolling through firefighters and watching* This Is Us *when you happened upon a handsome single doctor. Ninety-eight match percentage? A true angel, algorithm-sent.*

Spill your wine on anyone who asks how you met. There's no reason your busybody friends need to butt into your private life!

Divert attention to your friend's divorce. If Sheila starts judging you for meeting someone in real life, remind her that *her* Hinge marriage lasted a mere two years. That'll show her!

Claim you were on a digital detox. Use simple words they'll understand, like "unplug" and "Gwyneth" and "data breaches that Facebook did nothing to stop and resulted in foreign powers manipulating our political processes because Mark Zuckerberg cares more about personal profit than behaving ethically."

Sleep with Janie's boyfriend. This is a great way to remind the whole friend group that not *all* the people you meet on Bumble are perfect.

Dump them for someone you met on Tinder. It's not too late to find someone online. So call off the engagement and start responding to a few "U up?" messages. This is probably the easiest way to avoid having to explain to your friends that you were enough of a loser to meet someone in real life.

(originally seen on newyorker.com)

Once, I voluntarily went on a second date at a comic book museum in New York City. You may wonder how much I'd have to like a person to go to a comic book museum with them—quite a lot, usually. But this was a *second* date. With early dating, we're often so caught up in the excitement of a new person that we go with the flow. If you've gone on eight boring first dates and finally meet someone who makes you laugh, maybe you turn a blind eye to some of their quirks, like the fact that they have six hairless guinea pigs. Maybe you even hide who you are initially, and you pretend to *love* hairless guinea pigs, to show them you're compatible. And maybe before long, you've actually adopted two of their hairless guinea pigs because their landlord threatened to evict them for illegal pet ownership, but anyway, this isn't the story of how I came to be the mother of Fluffy and Dandruff.

During early dates, some of us let the rules take over—don't have sex too soon, don't text too much, don't ask if you can borrow their Roomba—in the hopes we'll get to a place where we don't have to play by the rules anymore. Others see it as a chance to throw caution to the wind in a low-stakes environment—they may never see you again, so why bother with niceties? Either way, early dating is strange and exhausting, but I've learned a lot from it. Mostly about Batman, but still.

Quiz

Is Your Dating Style More Carrie, Samantha, Charlotte, Miranda, or Henry—the Fruit Fly I Can't Get Out of My Kitchen?

1. Your preferred dating app is:

a. Hinge. I want a wide variety of Aiden-lookalikes.

b. Tinder. I *like* that it's a sex app. Less talking, more me being on top, touching my own clit, getting off, getting myself off, etc.

c. eHarmony. I'm looking for something serious, like a trust fund.

d. The League. The perfect app for the career-obsessed. For example, lawyers must date other lawyers—it's the only way to get people to date lawyers.

e. Farmers Only. Love a good compost bin.

2. Your opening line is:

a. Heyyyy don't Google me.

b. Send nudes.

c. Hi! I'm Charlotte, it's so wonderful to meet you. I have to admit I'm not used to online dating—I'm really a traditionalist, but I wanted to start thinking outside the box. How long does it take you to complete the Tuesday *New York Times* crossword puzzle?

d. If you've ever been arrested in the State of New York, I will find out.

e. Bzzzz.

3. Your ideal first date is:

a. At a "hip" club downtown.

b. In my bedroom, because I'm a kinky little minx. Saucy saucy grrrr.

c. At my parents' country club in Greenwich, ideally with one of their business colleagues present to oversee the proceedings.

d. At a library.

e. Inside a banana peel. In the trash or in the sink—I'm flexible.

4. Your favorite cocktail is:

a. A pink one.

b. Also a pink one.

c. I'm going to have to go with "a pink one," too.

d. A tie between a pink one and the Bar Exam.

e. That one spot on the counter you forgot to wipe. Mmmmm, canta-loupe.

5. The best time to have sex is:

a. Not sure, but I will devote 5,000 words to figuring it out.

b. Constantly constantly constantly. I do exactly one thing and one thing only—make money, buy clothes, and fuck.

c. Exactly nine months before I want to give birth to our daughter, Pres-tiginiana.

d. A quickie anytime I have a free five minutes. I'll take breaks when corporate greed does!

e. The moment you enter the room. It's show time—you'll see us mul-tiplying on that bag of grapes you left out. You'll make a note-to-self to keep grapes in the fridge next time, but will you ever remember?

6. What quality are you most looking for in a romantic partner?

a. Excitement! So that I can sell a story about it.

b. Big shlong

c. Someone who wears plaid and will love me forever

d. A guy who gets that, unlike other women, I *work*. And *think*.

e. Someone who can resist the temp-tation of vinegar. Trying to get rid of me? Impossible—no one keeps me out of the kitchen.

7. What is your job?

a. Writing about *dating*

b. Samantha Jones, Public Relations. Oh, sorry, wait, did I give away the answer to the quiz?

c. I work at an art gallery, but I suppose the thing I do that earns me "income" is being a daughter.

d. I'm a lawyer. Duh. That's why my hair is short.

e. I professionally shame people into wiping down their countertops constantly. Constantly. *Constantly.*

8. You'll know you're ready to move in together when:

a. It works with my personal narrative.

b. I'm spending more time commuting to their apartment than *being fingered.*

c. I turn 30. I'm currently 33.

d. I get knocked up. I don't have time to think about these questions, I'm a lawyer.

e. I've only got one honeydew rind left, and it looks like you just went to the farmers' market.

9. Your fairy princess wedding dress is:

a. White. Because I like to push the envelope, but not that far. Actually, not at all.

b. Low-cut with a long slit down my leg. I'd like to be able to have sex without taking it off, if possible, because I'm busy, and I like to fuck.

c. Expensive and traditional, fitting for whatever my future spouse's culture may be.

d. A pantsuit.

e. This is actually an insensitive question, as fruit flies are not legally allowed to wed, and also you just swatted down one of my girlfriends. I know I have 400 other options, but she was my favorite. Is having a clean kitchen worth breaking my heart?

10. You know a relationship is over when:

a. They leave you a Post-it, like a scared little boy.

b. You—*not* them—cum.

c. Their mother has sent you divorce papers.

d. I'm a little busy. Like, reading.

e. Never. I never leave, no matter how many times you wipe down the counters. I'm here for good. You're stuck with me forever, honey. Speaking of which....mmmm, honeydew.

Results:

Mostly a's: Carrie! You steer the ship of the show and the relationship, at least enough to make it palatable on paper.

Mostly b's: Who could have seen this coming—Samantha Jones. You like *sex*, and you like it *now*, but if you can't get it *now*, then you like it *later*. Nice.

Mostly c's: A classic Charlotte. You're looking for The One, but if you can't find that, you'll settle for a One (out of 10) if he has a lot of money. If that sounds bad, just remember—you have perfect hair.

Mostly d's: I'm sorry to say that you're a Miranda. The lawyer.

Mostly e's: Henry—the fruit fly I can't get out of my kitchen. You may be annoying, but you did win.

Is the Third Date Too Soon to Have Sex for the Third Time?

If you're interested in having sex for the third time on the third date, it's important to ask yourself if it's too soon. There are an indeterminate number of variables to consider, including but not limited to: the type of sex, the sex position, what direction your head would be facing during said sex, your astrological sign, your mother's maiden name, and why *Scrubs* decided to have a ninth season.

I can't say for sure whether or not the third date is too soon to have sex for the third time, but it's *definitely* too soon to have sex for the third time in the same pair of socks you wore the second time.

If both prior sex instances occurred on the second date, the third date may be an appropriate time to do it for the third time. However, if there was one sex on the first date and one sex on the second, you need to space things out a bit—wait until in between the third and fourth dates to do a third sex. Use that newfound free time on the third date to really drill into their stance on ATM fees.

Finger stuff on the third date is fine in any and all circumstances, as long as you've used Purell.

The most important thing is that by the eighth date, you've had sex seventy-four times. This is the key to a successful, long-term relationship and also a UTI. Seventy-five is way too many. Seventy-three is never enough.

A sex session can occur before the second date, but if you want it to happen *on* the second date, you're going to have to respond to the text they sent after the first. It can also occur anytime before 2 p.m. or after 2:07 p.m., but not in between, unless you're willing to shout your dirty talk over the sound of a lawn mower.

Sex on the first date is tricky—I never know whether to do it before or after. I'd say if you're confused, wait until the ninth date or until you've opened up a joint checking account together, whichever comes last.

Don't ever double-text someone you've slept with. If they send you 15 texts in a row about how their apartment just got robbed and they need a place to crash, respond, "k," or else you'll come off too eager. If they then ask what your address is, give them just the house number and wait for them to ask what street—you don't want to look desperate. The moment you sleep with someone, you have to stop caring about whether or not their livelihood has been snatched from them, unless you want to appear pathetic.

A little to the right, if you don't mind. You'll get it soon, though. And thanks. Sorry, I just wanted to give you an example of what may happen if you do a 2:04 p.m. sex.

If you're looking for casual sex, say that. If you're looking for serious sex, don't say that. Never, ever, ever, ever—not even at your wedding. Don't ever use the word "serious," not even in another language. It spooks people.

Oral sex on the second date is totally fine as long as it is *not* with the person you're on a date with. Obviously.

You can't sleep with anyone who's ever slept with any of your friends. Not because of loyalty, but because they all have terrible taste. Why so many method actors?

Also, unrelated, change your socks.

Listen to what your high school sex-ed teacher always told you. *If you have to go to the bathroom in the middle of class, raise your hand first.*

Don't sleep with multiple people at once. You have a twin-sized bed; no one will wake up feeling refreshed.

Always have the outercourse before the dessert course.

Ghosting after a one-night stand is completely inappropriate in all states except those that begin with the letter *P*, and it's even illegal in states that begin with the letter *Q*. It's only acceptable if you actually die. Still, his friends will probably talk shit about you before or after but not *during* your funeral. I mean, I said it was acceptable, not polite.

If you have to break up with a sex buddy, do it at a Trader Joe's, so at least they can get a free sample after. Don't ever do it over the phone. If you insist on doing it over text, wait until you know they're in a Trader Joe's. If you don't live anywhere near a Trader Joe's, move.

And never have phone sex, especially if you have an iPhone 11 Pro Max. It's much too big.

What My First Date Means by "Quirky"

If you're anything like me, you've been called "quirky" more times than you can count (which is a bummer, because one of my quirkiest qualities is that I *love* counting). I'm not sure what alerts them to this trait—I think texting a first date at 6:15 a.m. to confirm is *organized*. "Quirky" is one of those statements that's not *really* a compliment, but not quite an insult, either.* Here's what I assume they actually mean:

- Weird, but bangably so

- Has bangs

- Shares a first name with a classic quirky actress (examples: Zooey, Natalie, Anyone with Short Hair, Zooey)

- Odd, but I'm unwilling to figure out how

- Odd, but I'm willing to ignore . . . for now

- Socks mismatched. Alternatively, one sock not present.

- Does not align with my preexisting idea of what she should be like. Disconcerting.

- Makes her own kombucha. Or at the very least, coffee.

- Will inevitably pressure me to start a garden

- Sometimes sad

- Substantially more interesting than me. This is intimidating.

- Wears a scarf

- Difficult to compliment in a more specific way

- Carries a backpack . . . as an adult

- Fun but probably temporary

- Weird, and not even in a bangable way

*Update: It's been confirmed that this is actually an insult.

Headlines of *Atlantic* Articles I Only Read Because Someone Particularly Attractive Sent Them to Me after a First Date

THE CASE FOR GOING ON A SECOND DATE
WITH SOMEONE WHO ASSIGNS YOU HOMEWORK
ON THE FIRST DATE

THE PROFOUND, UNDYING STUPIDITY OF
ASSUMING THAT READING THIS ARTICLE
WILL HELP US CONNECT

THE SMART WAY TO FIX MY HINGE PROFILE
SO I DON'T ATTRACT THE KIND OF PERSON WHO
ASSUMED I WANT TO READ THIS

A BRIEF HISTORY OF MY ROMANTIC LIFE,
INCLUDING HOW MANY OF THESE ARTICLES I'VE
READ TO TRY TO CONVINCE MY DATE I'M SMART

WILL THE BRITISH PARLIAMENT PERMANENTLY
CHANGE MY WILLINGNESS TO WASTE
TWO HOURS READING ABOUT UK POLITICS TO
IMPRESS SOMEONE MILDLY HOT? LIKE,
IF THEY'RE A SEVEN, BUT NOWHERE NEAR AN
EIGHT? SEVENS AND EIGHTS ARE THE TWO
FURTHEST APART—THE *ATLANTIC* SHOULD
EXPLORE THAT PHENOMENON INSTEAD

THE SECOND DATE COULD BE MUCH WORSE

CAN CREATIVE EDUCATORS FIND A WAY TO
HELP ME REMEMBER THE SPECIFICS OF THIS
ARTICLE FOR OUR SECOND DATE?

HOW THE LEFT MADE ME FEEL EVEN WORSE
WHEN YOU BAILED ON THE DATE I SPENT
HOURS PREPPING FOR

BILL O'REILLY, ELLEN DEGENERES,
MILEY CYRUS, SHIRLEY TEMPLE, MY MOM,
HERMIONE GRANGER, AND THE REASON
I STOPPED DATING PEOPLE WHO LIST THE
ATLANTIC AS ONE OF THEIR HOBBIES

What to Send after a Date to Say, "I Had Such a Great Time Last Night, Can I Borrow Your Roomba?"

> Hey! Last night was so fun, we should totally do it again sometime. Maybe you can come over to my place, although the floor is a bit dusty.

> Heyyyy!! Thanks for driving me home last night. You're super sweet and generous, which reminds me—you mentioned you had a Roomba?

> Great hanging out last night! You're a great conversationalist, and, even better, your jacket was so lacking in cat hair. Do you have some kind of device to keep things clean? If so, do you lend it out? At what stage in the relationship does that typically happen, would you say?

> Wow! Doing an escape room with you was fun! You just kept going and going and going—no matter how many walls you bumped into, you got the job done! You know what that reminds me of?

> I'd love to meet up again. Maybe on Sunday mornings? That's when I clean. Or, I guess, when I "cleaned"— before I had a handy little device to do it for me.

I loved talking to you, it was so considerate of you to generously offer up your Roomba. Well, I guess you didn't "offer" so much as begrudgingly sighed, "So I guess you'd like to borrow my Roomba?" after I'd spent 45 minutes explaining why my vacuum doesn't work—you were lucky to be on a first date with someone who knows how to fill the time. Anyway—I would!

Some days it's like, did you and I have fun, or did your Roomba and I have fun together? Hahahahahahahahah. It was me and your Roomba. Hope you didn't feel like you were third-wheeling! Because you were.

Hey babe, I loved your equipment. That Roomba I saw running all over your apartment is *chef's kiss*, and if you REALLY want to get in with me, you know what to do.

Does it really not turn off?

I went down on you for 45 minutes. That's 47 minutes longer than my past record. I think we're even.

Wait—do you want to go on a second date or do you want your Roomba back? Because yes to A and no to B.

I just want someone to talk to.

Also did I leave a bra in your car?

Dating in Your Twenties vs. Dating in Your Thirties

Sometimes, I feel like I'll do *anything* to meet a nice person. Except use dating apps, be friendly IRL, or leave my house. As the years pass, I get less and less excited about dating (and almost everything else). After all, a lot has changed.

Dating	20s	30s
What I'm Looking For:	I want a partner (relationship)	I want a partner (for chores)
Introductions:	Hey, I'm Ginny!	I'm Ginny.
Scheduling:	Do you want to meet at a bar downtown? Anytime is good for me!	I'll see you at 6:45 at the Fog on 9th and Spring. If you're not there by 6:47, I'm leaving. My bedtime is 10 p.m. on the dot.
First Date Conversation:	Let me tell you about my job.	Let me list every embarrassing and/or unhygienic fact about myself and see if you're still here when I'm done.

Dating	20s	30s
Hobbies:	Are you into brewing your own kombucha?	Are you in therapy? If not, explain yourself.
Following Up:	Heyyyyy I had fun last night! How's your week going?	What's your email, I will send GCal invite for second session.
Sex Stuff:	Oh that feels good!	Here's a 30-slide PowerPoint presentation on how to make me cum. I expect you to memorize it.
Getting Serious:	Yay I like you!	Fuck, I like you.
Breakups:	I don't know if this is going to work out, do you want to stay friends and maybe still sleep together every once in a while?	Please leave.

Other Topics to Bring Up When They Aggressively Put Your Lifestyle Choices on Blast by Asking If You Only Own One Bra

The rumors are *not* true. I own multiple bras, but only one is cute and functional. If you're in a similar situation, here's what to change the conversation to, should the topic come up:

- The weather

- What we're going to have for dinner

- What we're going to have for dinner tomorrow

- The many pairs of underwear you own, including the ones that are so ripped they now count as two separate pairs

- Laura Dern—she's always a good conversation topic. So much to say!

- Other examples of rude questions, aside from the one they just asked

- Sport(s). Just kidding—never bring up sport(s).

- What even *are* bras?

- Llamas

- Where they see this relationship going

- Where you see this relationship going

- Moving in together

- Future children

- Laura Dern, again, if you can't think of anything else to say

Outperform the Competition on a First Date with Me

- Show up.

- Don't be terrible.

- Have showered at some point in the last four days.

- Tip.

- Ask at least one personal question.

- Don't talk about how you hate animals.

- Don't say anything about any famous actress's plastic surgery.

- Don't say anything so egregiously bad that I waste the next eight days thinking about how much I hate you.

- Don't ever wear cargo shorts.

- Lend me your Roomba.

- Don't send me a 4,500-word *Atlantic* article the next day.

- Don't ask me anything.

- Don't call me "quirky."

And voilà! You're in the top 99 percent. Congratulations and, also, sorry (to me).

What I'm Looking For

I'm looking for a partner who listens extremely closely to everything I say; but if I say something stupid, they forget it immediately.

I'm looking for a partner who is super clean but also totally okay with the fact that my apartment is covered in a layer of filth. And also, they're willing to clean it very quickly and without complaint.

I'm looking for a partner who's very opinionated but has no firm opinions, except the ones I give them.

I'm looking for a partner very hot but not appealing to anyone else. I don't want them turning any heads but mine. Actually, don't turn my head either, I have chronic neck pain.

I'm looking for a partner passionate about their career but willing to drop it at a moment's notice if mine becomes more important, which it is.

I'm looking for a partner who's obsessed with me but also doesn't really care. Like, leave me alone when I want you to, duh. But also like and comment on everything I post. But not like, in a Reply Guy type way. Do it tastefully, but constantly.

I'm looking for a partner who's allergic to cats so we can use it as an excuse to never visit my Aunt Grace, but who also loves cats so they're willing to care for the six I already own.

I'm looking for a partner who's available but never around. I'm busy.

I'm looking for a partner tall but short. Tall, so I can look up at them, but short, so they get what it's like to be short.

I'm looking for a partner who wants to settle down because I'm at the point where I know exactly what I want and I see myself with a family and stability, but I'm also looking for a partner who wants to live in a new city every year and is willing to handle all the logistics of our constant moves.

Most of all—I'm looking for a partner who never, ever, ever points out hypocrisy.

Managing technology and your dating life simultaneously is a full-time job—honestly, we should get dental insurance. Texting is a wonderful way to take the anxiety of an IRL social interaction and make it last all day. Typing paragraphs, pages, and whole diaries into a device that saves them permanently is nothing short of heroic. It's also a recipe for disaster. Is it any wonder people argue over text when you can't see the other person's facial expression? If we become dependent on Instagram for validation, why *wouldn't* we be mad that our partner hasn't liked our most recent post? And why is the guy I'm casually seeing Venmo-ing some random person for eggplant parmesan—he's clearly lying to me about being lactose intolerant.

I'm willing to bet that anyone who claims their relationship to their phone is uncontentious doesn't actually have a phone. The longest I go without checking my phone is when I'm talking on it. And it's not just time-consuming, it's hard! Texting and social media come with their own set of ever-changing rules. When I was twenty-seven, I dated a thirty-two-year-old who didn't know you could see who'd viewed your Instagram stories (literally, educate yourself). My sister is five years younger than me and claims that Snapchat is, one, only for your side pieces, and two, about to replace the *New York Times*. It's impossible to keep up, and you're almost certainly going to be confused, or worse—anxiously awaiting a potential text from someone who might never respond.

You've probably found that technology vastly overcomplicates your love life. Still, you've become so dependent on Google Maps (whether or not you can see the street names, which you can't) that giving up your phone just isn't going to happen, so you may as well find a way to laugh about it.

Alternatives to the Three-Day Rule of Texting

The three-day rule of texting says you should give someone three days after a date to text you back. After that, you can give up on expecting to hear from them and curse their name in perpetuity. Three days, though? It's *unbelievable* that there are still people doing this. Three days is enough time to go viral, conceive a baby, exercise once, and watch three Netflix series—it's a lifetime.

With technological advances and the deterioration of my personal patience, I now expect my dates to text significantly faster. Waiting three days is canceled. The following alternatives to the three-day rule outline what events can occur and how much time can elapse without my date texting me, before I declare the relationship over.

The 7-Minute Rule: If you haven't texted within seven minutes of my leaving your house, you clearly don't care whether or not I made it to my UberPool quickly enough to evade the cancellation fee, and I'm just not down to be with someone that selfish.

The 4-Subtweet Rule: Look, I'm going to subtweet you on the way out of your apartment (barring exceptional, life-threatening circumstances like my phone being out of battery). And I'm going to subtweet you again when I get home. And probably the next time I pee. But if I make it to a fourth subtweet—"guys who still think the pull-out method works are canceled"—and *you* haven't pulled out your phone to ask if it was me who looked at your LinkedIn seventeen times, then *you're* canceled.

The 6-Minutes-of-Browsing-Self-Help-Books Rule: If I've had time to check out self-help books online for more than six minutes before you've checked in, don't even bother. Once I read *Why You Don't Need a Man or Carbs*, I'm going to be so over you *and* your lasagna that I stole from your fridge. So you better ask if I want to get dinner this week and/or if I followed your cousin on Instagram *before* my browsing is done—you won't get the chance after. And yeah, I followed a *few* of them. Sorry.

The 2-Taylor-Swift-Album Rule: Yes, I understand that she puts out albums at a startling pace, so if one comes out before you've had a chance to text me, I don't blame you. I mean, she only gave seventeen hours' notice for *folklore*—she could feasibly drop one and then announce it the next day. But if we get to a *second* album and you haven't had the decency to ask if it was me who reported your Hinge profile to get you kicked off the site—well, you're just not communicative enough for me to give you my time.

The 3-IG-Story Rule: If you've had time to post three Instagram stories but you haven't had time to text me, "Hey, how'd you get my sister's address?"—it's *over*.

The 8-Therapist-Voicemails Rule: You've given me so much time that I've left my therapist *eight* voicemails about how every time I sleep with someone new, they immediately pull away, I just don't know what's wrong with me, they seem unwilling to talk about engagement rings or our future joint checking account even though it's been three weeks, will anyone ever love me like that teddy bear did, etc. Consider my love *withdrawn*.

The 5-Nervous-Breakdowns Rule: It's okay if I have one nervous breakdown (glorified crying, TBH, which is an unglorified orgasm, IMO) before you text me. And then it's okay if I have three more. I am an adult woman who is overwhelmingly proud of herself if she brews coffee without setting off the fire alarm, so, yeah, sometimes breakdowns *happen*. But if I get to my *fifth* nervous breakdown, and you haven't so much as texted me asking if I told your mom that I'm your girlfriend, then I will *never* be your girlfriend (unless you, like, ask me to).

The 900-Word-Email-About-the-Futility-of-Dating Rule: When I get home from your apartment, I may have some thoughts about the social custom we call "dating." And I may begin to put them in an email to a close friend, distant friend, professional acquaintance, college kickball team mailing list, or your paternal grandfather. However, if this email grows so long it includes references to Gloria Steinem, Esther Perel, and Lana Del Rey—we're through.

The Burning-Your-Name-in-Effigy-Cursing-the-Moment-We-Met-Creating-a-Voodoo-Doll-of-You-That-I-Won't-Use-But-Will-Keep-Forever 3-Day Rule: Sorry, but if you waited three full days you kinda asked for it?

Phantoms and Prejudice

It is a truth universally acknowledged that "playing the dating game" involves abandoning any and all sense of dignity. As the second-eldest daughter of the Bennets, Lizzie Bennet bore the family's responsibility to marry well. Lizzie herself did not have need of such gentlemen, and if she did, she certainly did not have need of ones who behaved like this.

And yet, it was Mr. Darcy who had won her affection. It was he who she'd initially rebuffed so firmly, who had ultimately persisted. And now, she could not help but confess that she was expecting him to send a letter—she'd been expecting it since Sunday.

At length, it occurred to her perhaps a letter from Mr. Darcy was unacceptably late. She raised her brow squarely at me from across the drawing room.

"I pray you tell me the reason for your joyous visit," she said, joylessly.

Indeed, I was an odd addition to the Bennet household. I'd been sent from the year 2022 to explain one simple, frustrating phenomenon to the charming Bennet sisters. Lizzie had believed she would hear from her suitor, Mr. Darcy, by now, but no message had arrived. Confusion had rippled through the household, and it was I who was to reveal what had transpired. You see, this was the 1800s. The Bennet women didn't yet know about . . . *this*. I took a deep breath.

"So, okay, Lizzie—you know how you wrote Darcy a letter? And you usually get one back within a fortnight?"

"Yes, give or take several days should a steed fall ill and die."

"Right, well, sometimes people you're dating will get your letter, and then they just . . . stop sending one back. Like, they don't want to keep dating, but they don't know how to say so, so they just ignore you. It's called 'ghosting' because it's like he just disappeared. Like a ghost."

"Ghosts? Like all my closest friends?" Kitty, the second youngest Bennet, asked. "I should surely allow the kind Mr. Darcy to play—"

"Leave the ghosts be," said Mrs. Bennet. "They are as welcome in Longbourn House as you." I would have preferred Lizzie's mom not be there when I had to tell her she was being de facto dumped in the most cowardly way possible; but, alas, it wasn't my choice. When there's nothing to do but sit about a drawing room all day, rejection becomes a family affair.

"No, Kitty," I said. "Mr. Darcy's not a ghost—he's just doing what we now call 'ghosting.' Not responding."

Aghast, Lizzie stared into my eyes, directly and not entirely without cruelness. "He's not going to write? He didn't want to write, and so he did not? That's preposterous, and thoroughly unbefitting of both ghost and man."

"Yeah, he's not responding. You'd know by now if he were."

"We should be generous in our spirits and give him several days," Jane, the eldest Bennet sister, offered, unhelpfully. In the habit of doing it more than she ought, Jane found it fitting to weigh in. "Let us be optimistic and pray that it was a mere death in his household. These types of things are a bit more common in our time than yours."

I rolled my eyes. She was trying to guilt me with the "You-don't-get-it-because-you're-from-the-future-where-people-don't-just-die-all-the-time" shtick, and I wasn't having it.

"Jane, you're naïve," I said. "Hot girls shouldn't give dating advice."

"I simply don't think men treat women like this. It doesn't seem right. It's one thing to not let a lady own land or inherit her husband's wealth, but to plainly stop responding to her messages?" Lizzie said. "I just won't believe it."

How could I get through to Lizzie? She had to move on with her life. Surely there must be . . . some other neighbor she could fall for. Someone else must have a farm, or some green hills or something. "Guys just do that. Women do, too. We've just put a name on it in the twenty-first century, but it's been happening forever. It's also a coward's way out. They say they want to hang, and then they'll stop responding."

"Mr. Darcy's not like other guys," Lizzie said. "He's fictional."

I got her point, but at this stage in my dating life, I'd stopped trusting any of them, fictional or not. The Bennet sisters seemed horrified to hear about 2022, and I felt it was my duty to calm them, in whatever way I could.

"Don't worry, you can have jobs and vote and own property," I said. "Plus, processed food."

"I'd like to stay in 1813, I should think," Jane asserted. "It's nicer here."

"Wait till you try Sun Chips," I said.

"He wouldn't just *not respond*," said Mrs. Bennet. "My entire life's purpose is to see my daughters married, and even *I* think that's unfair."

Indeed, Darcy's behavior stood out as bad in a world in which women could only advance their social standing through marriage to a wealthy man. And look—as a lady who mostly dates aspiring comedians who don't floss, I kinda got it. Women will put up with a lot.

"Look, Lizzie," I said. "This is a Jane Austen novel. Everyone is just sitting around all day. If he wanted to write you, he would have written you. He had no other plans."

I didn't want to be harsh, but I needed to reach her. "What was your last interaction with the Darce-ster like?"

Lizzie furrowed her brow. "He seemed distant. But then again, he oft does."

The entire room nodded collectively.

"I know, right," I said. "He really needs to get over it and go to therapy for the whole dead-parent thing. Like, get a hobby and take responsibility for your actions, Darcy. How long are you really going to be his Prozac, Liz?"

"What's Prozac?" the ladies asked in unison.

"Ah, yet another wonderful thing about 2022. I'd happily share mine, but it takes a few weeks to kick in. But anyway, Lizzie—was he *more* distant than usual?"

"Are we quite sure he didn't just have the decency to die?" Jane asked. She was uniquely unable to wrap her mind around his behavior (yet another hot girl problem—thinking all guys are good).

Mary, the middle, boring Bennet, arose from her chair and took a seat at the piano. She began to play Mozart's Requiem in D Minor. A beautiful, haunting song. Haunting, almost like—

"A ghost!" Lizzie exclaimed. I'd reached her. Mr. Darcy wasn't going to write back. "I'm so sorry to say it, but our odd and somewhat-unwelcome visitor is right! Darcy is acting like a ghost! He's shown no regard for the moral standards of this society! He's no better than Lydia!"

The sisters now turned to Lydia, their youngest. She shrugged. They made a good point.

"His arrogance, his conceit, his selfish disdain—" Lizzie was worked up.

"Dating sucks," I said. "I went on two incredible dates with this Argentinian painter, and then I asked if she wanted to meet my mom, and she just stopped responding."

Mrs. Bennet was horrified. "You didn't invite her to meet your mother on the first date?"

"No—"

"Perhaps *that's* why she ghosted," the Lady of the House said resolutely.

Lizzie had stopped paying attention. "Every day confirms my belief in the inconsistency of all human characters, even fictional ones. To think, I ever considered staking my entire family's livelihood on him! Or worse, kissing! He is dead to me."

And then, just as Lizzie had committed to burning Mr. Darcy's name in effigy, he appeared in the doorway. His countenance was sober. He was taciturn in the best of times, and when he entered upon a room that had very obviously just been speaking ill of him, he was silent. He really *did* need Prozac.

"Were you just uttering my name?" he asked.

"You didn't write," Lizzie said plainly. "I feared—"

"My carriage driver had consumption. Once I hired a new one, I decided it would be expedient to appear in person. What did you fear?"

"I thought it was possible . . . but no, of course not," Lizzie said. She flashed a look at me, an angry one, one that said, *you stupid future idiot.* She pointed at me. "*She* said you didn't want to tell me you weren't coming, so you'd just disappear, and not write. Stop responding."

"You thought I would do what!?" Darcy said. "A lady's imagination is very rapid. That I would just *say nothing*? And that's how I'd end our romantic engagement?"

"It's not my fault—our visitor, she said two hundred years in the future, people sometimes just 'ghost,' and you'd never know why. But I should never have believed her—I was foolish."

"You must allow me to tell you how ardently I think this ghostly habit is stupid."

"Is the carriage driver dead?" Mrs. Bennet asked, but the conversation had drifted.

"Ah, Mr. Darcy, how silly I was to dismiss you! Of course you love me, how could you not? I'm spunky and opinionated—that's my thing! And moody men love that! We shall happily be miserable by one another's sides forever!"

Darcy and Lizzie embraced, as her sisters stared jovially into the back of her neck. It seemed things were settled. But I wasn't satisfied.

"You should have texted, Darce," I said. The Bennet sisters may have forgiven him, but I certainly had not.

People Who Actually *Did* Lose Their Phones

Have you ever told a friend that their date "may have lost their phone"? If so, you were lying to make her feel better, and that's an important part of friendship. But then again . . . were you lying? Contrary to popular belief, there actually *are* people out there who *have* lost their phones—or are even whimsical enough to let them die—and it's time to tell their stories.

It was October 2017. Twenty-two hours after a charming date at a quaint East Village bar (the only place to get a Manhattan cocktail under $18), Jennifer texted Brent "wyd?" Brent would have responded, at least to find out what "wyd" meant. Sadly, his phone slipped out of his hands on the subway track and was lost to the 6 train, forever. Jennifer would spend the next forty-five minutes checking her texts before sadly turning to her next Tinder match, the one currently in bed with her.

On a cold winter's day, Mark left his house with his phone in the butt of his jeans. He'd gone on three dates with Chris and found them absolutely not-bad. Chris had texted that morning to confirm their plans for that night. Mark should never have put the phone in his back pocket—it was quickly swiped from behind. Sadly, he couldn't respond to confirm his plans with Chris, even though he did get SMS messages on his work and home laptops, because he didn't want to.

Darren enjoyed spending time with Felicia. She had a winning personality, and she'd never once (not once) asked, "Why don't you have toilet paper?" He texted her at 9 p.m. on a Tuesday, asking if she was available at 9:15. She would have responded, except she had tweeted "lol butts" to her nearly 20k Twitter followers. The tweet received 0 likes in two minutes. Zero. In the face of deep shame, she hurled her phone into the sea. Some people just don't get art. Darren never heard from her again. But he did have to laugh—butts, haha.

On February 2 at 4:19 p.m., Brenda asked Steve if he'd like to come over for dinner and "snuggling" that night. Steve never responded. Brenda later saw on the news that he'd killed seven men in a holdup at a nearby bank. Even worse— cops suspected it was premeditated. That meant he could have texted her to say he was busy. And that's how she knew he was an asshole.

Cynthia made the poor choice to tell Nadia that she loved her over text. Nadia wanted to say it back. Unfortunately, a crocodile ripped the phone from Nadia's hands, just as she was about to respond. She was brutally eaten alive, but it's quite clear that what happened to Cynthia was worse.

A Pitch Meeting for Read Receipts

Don: I have an idea—does everyone have a phone?

Everyone nods. Most people are on their phones.

Don: And does everyone hate their phone?

Everyone nods, looking sadly at their phones.

Don: Does everyone feel like their value as a human is determined by how many texts they get? Because it is?

Everyone nods, now squirming uncomfortably in their seats.

Don: Does everyone want to gouge their eyeballs out when they send a text and don't hear back?

Everyone nods. Some have even started to cry.

Don: Especially if it's to someone you're seeing romantically?

Everyone is staring at the ground. At this point, eye contact has become physically painful.

Don: And you had a nice third date, but there were definitely some stilted moments in the conversation when you had to wonder, Wait—did I just suggest I was a tax dodger? Because I was making a joke. Oh, god, they think I'm a horrible person. Shit. Shit. Shit. Okay. Let me change the topic. I'll ask about their mom. What if she's dead? What if they had two dads and I'm erasing that experience? Fuck. They just asked me a question, but I completely forgot what it was. I suck at everything. I'm going to go pee.

Two people leave the room, dramatically. You could cut the tension with a knife. Someone pulls out a knife.

Don: And then you push past that awkwardness and the rest of the evening goes okay. You even score a goodnight kiss, and they say they want to go out again, but you're not completely positive. Like—what if they were being polite? Did you pressure them into saying you wanted to go out again? Are you a monster? You must text them to confirm they don't hate you. Except, they haven't responded in two hours, so it seems likely that they do hate you, and you now take this opportunity to relive every awkward comment you made on the date? Ugh—maybe you *are* a tax evader!

Someone makes a yelping sound, like what a puppy would do if you stepped on its tail.

Don: And as you await their response, you become unable to focus on anything else in your life. You forget to water your plants, because you're so busy trying to convince yourself their phone died, or they never saw the text, or there was some extenuating circumstance that caused them not to text? Your apartment is now covered in dry leaves.

Everyone has essentially melted into puddles of despair on the floor. One woman throws her phone at the window with gusto, but the glass doesn't shatter. The phone bounces off it and hits a man in the head. He's lucky enough to be knocked unconscious.

Don: What if we could take *that* feeling . . . and make it so much worse.

Everyone who is still left in the room is effectively catatonic, sobbing. The man who was hit with the phone may be dead—it's not possible to know.

Don holds up his hands dramatically, as if he's writing across the sky.

Don: Introducing read receipts—so you know, beyond a shadow of a doubt, that you're being ignored.

A Message in a Bottle

July 7, Midday: My dearest Federico! Fair tidings! Mother tells me your caravan is on the far side of the vast sea. If my calculations are to be trusted, this bottle should reach you within three weeks, assuming you're standing at exactly the same dock you were when I sadly departed, and assuming the wind continues to blow at exactly .87 knot/hour at 43 degrees north for the duration. I wanted to write to tell you that I miss you so dearly, and I cannot wait until our sweet reunion. Our night together meant so much to me—I treasure the squirrel's skin you gave me. I sleep with it in my bonnet.

July 8, Sunset: Federico, my most sincere apologies for the double bottle, but I fear I may have been hasty with the assumption that the wind would continue blowing in the same direction. Silly me—getting so caught up in my emotions, yet again. You're right—I'm *such* a girl. To ensure my bottle reaches you safely, I've sent fourteen bottles with the same message. Shall we reconvene below the orange tree near that fisherman's hut where we first met? In two weeks' time?

July 14, The Time of Evening When the Cattle Become Restless: Federico—I beg you to make haste with your response. Father insists we pack up this settlement and set sail for new lands before the fall equinox. I worry I may never see you again, unless your bottle washes to shore imminently. It is my good fortune that I should be able to see it from miles away—praise be that the Earth is flat.

July 16, The Period Betwixt Eating Oats and Watching the Apple Tree Grow: Fed—I shall assume your bottle got blown too far south, so neither of us has to feel guilty for the lack of response. Or that yours may have shattered. I know you use an Android bottle—is the screen even insured? See you tomorrow, I pray! My dear heart beats every moment for you! And for the sake of circulating my blood, which is something I've deduced from my girlish studies into human biology.

July 16, Five Minutes Later, Apple Tree Has Not Grown Noticeably:
HOPE*** not pray. I had said "pray" in my last bottle but I remember what you said about praying—the man whose face is framed upon your wall said it's the opiate of the masses, right, right, right. You're so smart!!

July 21, Dawn, I May Think: Federico! I stood in wait beneath the orange tree for hours and hours. Or perhaps minutes, I have no way to tell time. But you didn't arrive. Never you mind, though, I shall be beneath the orange tree again tomorrow. And the next day and the next day. Only because of the scheduling conflict, not because my heart is tainted with an obsession or the devil or anything super needy like that.

July 23, Sad Dusk: I don't mean to blow up your shores with these glass bottles, but it seems that you're being just a bit distant right now. Emotionally, that is. Geographically, I'm totally not mad that there's, like, an ocean between us. I mean, it's not your fault. If you could maybe light a fire somewhere on a hill? To show me you're still into this—I feel like I've given you plenty of chances to say you're not. Oh, and light it away from any wayward sheep, to spare their lives.

July 23, Sadder Dusk: You could at least send an "LOL" or something. This silence is getting kind of rude. I sacrificed a sheep in your honor last night. And you know I like sheep.

July 23, Saddest Dusk: I wish there were an "edit" feature so I didn't have to keep rebottling these notes. I swear I'm barely thinking about you.

July 23, How Long Does Dusk Last?: You know Beth has consumption, right? I'm just saying, if she's the reason . . .

July 25, Hour at Which I Set the Ground Grass Out for the Cows: Got your bottle. Sorry I came off too "needy." Yeah, I get it, it was just one night, but I figured the squirrel hide meant something. I didn't realize you'd just wanted help composting. Rest assured I won't be sending more bottles a-sail in your direction.

July 27, Tea Time: Did you just send me *Infinite Jest* in a 128-ounce bottle? Ew.

The Only Valid Reasons for Not Texting Me

It's okay if you don't text me. Actually, no; it's not. However, under *some* circumstances, I can understand how you *might think* it's okay to not swiftly pen me a response, including:

- Respecting my desire to be on my phone less.

- Not being able to think of a sufficiently witty reply.

- Being dead from something funny I said.

- Spending every single second with me IRL. In this case, it's *okay* to not text, but I'd prefer if you took your phone to the bathroom with you. Actually, I'll just come in the stall, it's easier that way.

- Being too busy at work. I've never dated a guy who took his job seriously, but I'm open to the possibility that it's somewhat taxing to "open up people's bodies" and "save their lives." Just don't make your job a full-time thing.

- Going off the grid on a silent, technology-free meditation retreat. That's hot. But try to pack your phone, if you can.

- Being in a relationship with my sister. Stop texting me, Steve.

- Emailing me instead because you wanted to write more.

- Calling me instead, just to hear my voice.

- Sending a carrier pigeon instead because you wanted me to know you care so much about me, you trained a pigeon. It shat all over me, though, so I would appreciate an apology text.

- Showing up at my door instead because you like me so much you paid one of those online services to give you my address. Also, you wanted to apologize for any havoc the pigeon may have wreaked on my apartment.

- A llama waltzed by and ate your phone. It happens, and I trust you, as long as you took a picture of it happening on your phone before the llama devoured it.

- Being a kitten. I understand that kittens can't text, in general. Well, *most* kittens. Like, if I knew of a kitten that *could* text, I would want it to text me. And I'd be mad if it didn't.

- Not having a phone because you're part of a government-funded study that tests whether or not phones ruin our brains. Actually, we got proof years ago that they do. I read about it, on my phone. Where's your phone? Text me back.

- Being one of the many people I didn't want to text me back. In this case, texting me is actually rude. Please infer from my vaguely dissatisfied facial expressions when I read your texts (which you can't see, you just have to imagine) that I don't want you to text me back.

- Being dead, but not from something funny I said. Like, having your heart not beat anymore, as confirmed by a doctor.

Sarah and Franco to Launch Their Relationship Online— A Press Release

Instagram, Sarah's Smartphone, June 6, 2022—Today, Sarah J., 27, and Franco P., 26, mark the official Instagram launch of their relationship. Sarah posted a photo to her Instagram of the two of them captioned, "This goon made me dinner," and Franco retweeted Sarah six times in a row. Sarah says six RTs aren't equivalent to a post, but she's generously chosen not to pick a fight. Sarah reports that she's saving her fight credits to use at Disney World.

The couple expects Sarah's post to earn about 140 likes on Instagram. She currently has 1,400 followers, and a 10 percent yield is in line with what she's seen of other similar couples in the past.

"If it's well under 120, it's because I've posted too many mirror selfies, and all my cousins have muted me," Sarah says. "So if that happens, at least I'll know to bring it up next Christmas."

Sarah and Franco have been seeing each other since January 2022, when they matched on Hinge. Sarah considers the official start date of their "thing" to be when Franco liked the photo of her holding a cat in one hand and a 40-oz of Miller Lite in the other, captioned, "I'm maternal." Franco dates the launch to three weeks later when they first had sex.

The soft launch of their public relationship occurred in March when Franco first put Sarah in his Instagram story. It was only the back of her head, however, because he was trying to tape a scene from *Twin Peaks.*

"I wanted to show my followers that I knew that the blue shoe in Season 1 Episode 7 was related to the murder in Season 2 Episode 9," he said. "Because a lot of people had questions about whether or not I knew that."

After a former coworker of Franco's DMed him to ask if he had a new "lady friend," Franco insisted that Sarah tell him if she saw the relationship going anywhere.

Specifically, to TikTok. He didn't want to be Tok'd without a little commitment. He later threatened to cut her off from his Disney+ if she didn't commit.

"A classic will-they-won't-they, a tale as old as time," Sarah said, of the conflict. "I don't even care about Disney+, but my friends describe it as a classic gateway drug to later being cut off from way better subscriptions, like HBO Max or the Criterion Channel."

"You like the Criterion Channel?" friends asked.

"No," said Sarah quickly.

Both of them say this is their first Instagram-official relationship, although Franco's college girlfriend Mallory disputes the claim.

"I put him in my Instagram story all the time," Mallory says, "but he didn't have an account, so I couldn't tag him. But he was definitely my boyfriend—we got matching STD tests."

Franco has not responded to her comment.

Sarah and Franco enjoy participating in a number of activities together, including smiling for photos, swiping through things on the internet, posting on the internet, and reading the internet. The two reside in Austin, TX, and co-own one cat, taken care of by Sarah's mother.

"Now that they're official on social media, can they take back the cat?" Mrs. J asks. "Sarah said it would be two weeks, tops, and it's now been six months. Some days, I wonder if she only got the cat for her Hinge profile."

The pair has not responded to her comment. The cat has not responded to our question regarding whether or not it was compensated for being Hinge content.

We wish all the best to these two lovebirds in their future endeavors!

Note: This press release was written by Do It for the Likes Unlimited, a PR firm that specializes in helping couples with the social media launch of a new relationship. We also handle breakups, taking a break, public rejections, and speed-eating contests.

Noncontroversial Responses for My Partner to Send to Any of My Texts, Regardless of the Content, in Case They're Confused and Need Some Ideas

- You're so right.

- Agreed.

- So pretty!

- Ahhh, has anyone ever told you you're a genius?

- Sorry.

- Of course they've told you you're a genius! Because you are a genius!

- I *like* that you don't use deodorant.

- Do you want my Hulu login?

- Do you want my Netflix login?

- Do you want my Pornhub login?

- Genius genius genius.

- See you soon, I already ordered fries.

Meet-Cutes for People Who Slid into Each Other's DMs

Meeting the right person can be easier than baking a cake from a box (which, to be fair, I've messed up many times). Sometimes, someone will twist their ankle "sliding" into your DMs, whether or not you're trying to use Instagram as a dating app. Still, it doesn't have to end badly. You might get some dick pics, but you also might get some really nice people (who possibly send really nice dick pics). Read on for heartwarming stories of couples who met via DM-slide.

We were followers for years before anything happened. I'd seen him around IG before, liking my friends' posts, occasionally commenting with the fire emoji. I'd always think—here's a guy who respects the flame of passion within women. Then, one day, it happened to me. I posted a picture of me and my sister at the beach, and he took the bait. I sent him a DM saying, "Hey Scott! Thanks for the fire brrrr I'm warm now!" We've been together ever since. He later revealed that emoji was intended for my seventeen-year-old sister, but he wasn't picky. Thank God.

 There was something in the way he misspelled "juise" that got my attention. The "c" is silent, anyway. I faved nine of his tweets in a row—that's about as hard as I'll come on to anyone. And it worked. The very next day, he was randomly wandering around right outside my apartment. Praise be for location tracking on Twitter. We've been together ever since.

Barry sent me four dick pics in a row, and I blocked him. They were definitely four different dicks. I then complained about it in my IG story, and a nice person DMed me to say, "Ugh, you are too beautiful for that to happen to you." We've been together ever since. I never asked if he thought average-looking people deserve unsolicited dick pics.

She was an early TikTok star. She had 4k followers, and I was lucky to be one of them—like getting in on the ground floor of Google. But a girl like that—she doesn't just date the first guy to post her TikTok vid to his Instagram story. No, she dates the first guy to do it five dozen times, so that's what I did. I lost 72 followers (87 percent) for her, because it turns out she's a famous conspiracy theorist, and my friends didn't love it. Blondes, they're full of surprises. Anyway, she and I have been together ever since. She now has 4.2k followers—I saw her when she was invisible.

She was cute on YouTube. She'd make these funny videos where she pretended to be a squirrel, just the most adorable impressions. When I couldn't find her on IG or Twitter, I scrolled through all her YouTube followers and found someone who appeared to be her mom. I asked for her number, and she gave it to me—I wish my mom were that chill. We met up. Turns out—those weren't impressions. We've been together ever since.

I saw her on the subway one time. She was checking her Facebook, but I've always been attracted to older women. I peered over her shoulder and got her name and friended her. Then, sent her a message asking her out. She responded that she only considered DM-slides on Instagram, so I found her there too. She ignored me, but it's okay, I'm married anyway. Wait—this is anonymous, right? Like, it won't say, "Submitted by Lloyd P. Wendelberry anywhere"—will it?

My parents never gave me the "sex talk." I still don't know what it is.

Oh, never mind, I just Googled it. Fun! Our earliest ancestors showed up on this planet without the ability to walk upright, form sentences, or use Incognito mode to stalk their exes, and yet they figured out how to keep the population going. That's because consensual sex—the only type that should exist and the type I'll be discussing in this chapter—if done correctly, can be pretty nice. But it does come with its fair share of complications. And miscommunication. And hurt feelings. And diseases. And also, UTIs. And also, stains (sorry, Mom, I really did like the sheets you got me).

Like everything else, sexual pleasure has been reshaped by our modern dating norms and technology. Truly, the saddest moment of my day is when I check my phone so soon after masturbating that I could still be enjoying the orgasm, if I weren't so addicted to Twitter. Anyway, no one has come to any sort of agreement on what sex means these days, and you might find yourself confused about where you stand with the person you're sleeping with. Sex is absolutely not required to have a very fulfilling relationship and/or life—nor are relationships necessary to have fulfilling sex—and there are undoubtedly some downsides. For one thing, it's sure to occupy a disproportionate amount of space in your mind. At least, it does for me.

It Happens with Bradley Cooper, and Other Inaccurate Things Rom-Coms Taught Me About Sex

Rom-coms gave me all kinds of inaccurate expectations about what adulthood would be like. For example, it looked fun. But in no area did rom-coms lead me astray more so than in the bedroom. My therapist once asked me if I used sex to get guys to like me ("No, not effectively," I said). But maybe I got that idea from the silver screen! My inaccurate assumptions about sex include the following:

- Over in six seconds, but with an outcome both people find satisfying

- Fully clothed

- Immediately followed by an "I love you"

- With a man I hated three scenes ago

- Orgasmic

- Exhausting

- Only once every ninety minutes

- At least once every ninety minutes

- You don't have a choice about falling asleep immediately after—you will

- In a one-bedroom apartment on the Upper East Side that I pay for on a freelance writer's "salary"

- Not followed by a waddle to the bathroom to avoid dripping and UTIs

- Vigorous, but not messy

- After I've eaten nothing but French fries for two weeks but without gas

- In Manhattan

- With Tom Hanks (again, heartbreak)

- The start of a relationship

- With someone hot (perhaps the biggest letdown of all)

- Very good

Indicate Sexual Interest to a Straight Man

- Say hello to him.

- Wave at him.

- Smile at him.

- Make eye contact with him.

- Make eye contact with the person sitting two chairs down from him.

- Have a profile on a dating app.

- Admit to knowing his name.

- Express that you're single, or at least don't affirmatively bring up a partner in every sentence. If you only mention your partner once every paragraph, then he may be confused as to whether or not you do in fact have a partner. Also, it's difficult to know where the paragraph breaks are in spoken conversation. Keep it to once per sentence.

- Drive a car. Guys are obsessed with cars.

- Wear makeup in his presence.

- Interact with any phallic objects in his presence, including but not limited to: a water bottle, a sunglasses case, a candle, a human body, your own arm (everything is phallic). And don't even get me started on eating a banana in the same room as him.

- Be married to his friend.

- Attend a party you *knew* he'd be at, as he texted you six times asking if you were going. Yes, the party was at your house, and you felt that it would be poor form to not invite everyone on your improv team, but still. Obviously you went because he went.

- Know even the tiniest bit about sports. Examples of facts that constitute flirting, if you know them: There's a ball in soccer. There's a ball in basketball. There's a ball in football. Balls are inherently sexual, because men have them.

- Breathe loudly.

- Breathe quietly.

- Aggressively assert a lack of sexual interest in him.

- Ignore him, but in a loud way.

- Be female in his presence. This is *always* a risk.

More Intuitive Meanings for the Phrase "Giving Head"

"Giving head" means having oral sex, which you'd know if and *only* if someone told you explicitly. Oral sex only involves a small percentage of your head—you just need your tongue and maybe one brain cell—so it's not clear why it's associated with the whole dang noggin. In fact, the term "giving head" would better apply to any number of other activities, including:

- Donating your hair.

- Using your actual skull to stop a leak.

- Passing out plastic skulls to children on Halloween. Make sure to also give them candy, or else you'll be the lamest house on the block.

- Donating your brain to science. Like Einstein, and probably a number of other men who thought all too highly of themselves.

- Beating your head against a wall to raise money for charity. First, make sure someone will sponsor you to do this, or else you're just killing brain cells for no reason.

- A pro-bono facelift.

- Selling Halloween masks.

- Some kind of taxidermy, but I don't like to think too much about it.

- Putting just the head of a chocolate bunny in an Easter basket. This is also a weird thing to do.

- The end of brain surgery where they put the skull cap back on. I've seen a lot of *Grey's Anatomy*, so I know exactly how it works. The person is without a head, and then Patrick Dempsey runs his hand through his hair and declares, "Give this man back his head!" Everyone applauds and fawns over him, except Meredith, who does love him but is distracted by something her mom said to her when she was six.

- Expressing your thoughts (actually, this is very similar to oral sex in that my sexual partners often stop me in the middle).

- Donating a portrait of someone, shoulders and up, to a museum.

- A head that gives you stuff. Like the Giving Tree, but a head, and less sad.

- Oral sex if you also use your nose and eyes and forehead and brain and ears.

- Oral sex if you get to keep the other person's head at the end. This would be weird. Not as weird as the chocolate bunnies, but still weird.

- Oral sex if you exchange heads at the end. This, I'd imagine, is what they mean by "reciprocation."

Nicknames for My Casual Sex Partners

Cute nicknames make sex better! It doesn't matter if you've met once or a ton of times (four)—use one of these fun monikers to enhance your love life.

LOML

Person I'm Definitely Dating

Person Who Causes My Friends to Say, "Oh, him, still?" When I Reference an Instance of Sex

Spouse

More Honest Meanings of the Phrase "Sexually Active"

I've been having sex regularly since college (#brag), and I've had a lot of different kinds (#bragagain). For example, I once slept with three guys in one weekend, although to be fair, it was a three-day weekend. Sure, I take the occasional thirteen-month break—who doesn't—but I'd say I'm "out there." But would I call myself "sexually active"? The dictionary defines *active* as "engaging in physically energetic pursuits." Physical? Energetic? No thank you. I usually really enjoy sex and want to please my partners, but I'm not over here pretending I'm some sort of Olympian. In fact, during sex, I typically get jealous of how many calories my partner is burning. Here are a few more accurate terms for what *I* do when I have sex:

- Sexually starting the sex

- Sexually present

- Sexually moaning, both intentionally and unintentionally

- Sexually giving very specific instructions while mostly just doing nothing

- Sexually lying there

- Sexually lying about why I can't move my leg

- Sexually having the sex

- Sexually telling not showing

- Sexually walking around my apartment naked with the curtains open

- Sexually wondering why sex can't be like it is in the movies (over in less than six seconds)

- Sexually being in the middle of sex

- Sexually learning we're actually nowhere near the middle

- Sexually actively avoiding activity

- Sexually *considering* being active but ultimately deciding against it. It just doesn't seem worth it to set a dangerous precedent like that.

- Sexually smiling. I just thought about *Little Women*. What an incredible film.

- Sexually planning what I'm going to tweet about the experience

- Sexually wondering what's for dinner

- Sexually having a ton of fun just lying here (truly) and wondering where people got the assumption that it's important to move

- Sexually trying to listen to your roommate's podcast in the background. I'm not sure I understand the point, though—it's just two people talking? About whatever? And they put it on the internet for people to hear? Who is bored enough to listen to this? Except me, but I'm in the middle of literally nothing. Oh, nice, did you cum?

- Sexually waiting to pee

- Sexually asking, "Are you almost finished?"

- Sexually following up with, "Just curious, not in a rush"

- Sexually stating that I'm a bit bored, but trying to be polite about it

- Sexually finishing the sex

- Sexually saying, "That was great"

- Sexually thinking, "That was great," because I love not moving

- Sexually wondering if enough time has passed to untangle

- Sexually dismounting

- Sexually checking my phone

- Sexually texting all my friends that I just did sex (nice)

Sex Positions That Are Particularly Weird to Hang Out in Once You're Done

No matter who you're having sex with, you may encounter someone who likes to "hang" in the sex position after it's completed. This can be a time to build intimacy, but it can also be a time to realize, Wait, this is well beyond my normal range of motion. Some positions are more awkward than others, including:

Doggie Style: I'm not sure I would ever have agreed to this position if I'd thought through the conclusion. Perhaps there's a reason dogs themselves never stop moving.

Leapfrog: If you're upright, your back will be tired. If you're bent over, you will pull a muscle. And if you don't—cool, we get it, you do "yoga."

Reverse Cowgirl: You better hope they have cool wall art and/or a cool back tattoo (depending on who is where).

Standing: I'm not, like, Jane Fonda. That's a lot of work! The sex itself was exhausting, and now I'm supposed to just *hang out* while *standing*?

Spooning: Can't stay in a spoon for too long, it makes me think of ice cream.

The Crab Walk: Ditto but about crabs.

69: Okay, you wanted it in your mouth but did you want it in your face?

Missionary: What am I supposed to do now, look at you? Do you know how many minutes of eye contact I can handle? Zero. None.

The Lotus: I will absolutely not do this sex position to begin with, so it's a moot point.

All of them: Sex is so awkward, and honestly, the five minutes post-coitus are so boring.

Masturbating alone: Actually, this one is nice. You can check your phone.

Having Sex Is Like Riding a Bicycle

Having sex is like riding a bicycle—you never forget how to do it.

Having sex is like riding a bicycle—it's important to use protection.

Having sex is like riding a bicycle—I was the only one not into it in college.

Having sex is like riding a bicycle—it makes you sweat.

Having sex is like riding a bicycle—a kickstand isn't necessary but does come in handy.

Having sex is like riding a bicycle—Scott is always an option.

Having sex is like riding a bicycle—everyone who's seen me do it has told me not to.

Having sex is like riding a bicycle—I always fall off.

Having sex is like riding a bicycle—only do it if you 100 percent want to.

Having sex is like riding a bicycle—it feels like all anyone ever talks about.

Having sex is like riding a bicycle—cars make it way more dangerous.

Having sex is like riding a bicycle—everyone else I know has done it by now.

Having sex is like riding a bicycle—I can never decide what speed is the most fun.

Having sex is like riding a bicycle—I aggressively lied to my whole class about having done it already.

Having sex is like riding a bicycle—it's totally fun and safe on your own, but then other people complicate it a lot.

Having sex is like riding a bicycle—I really want to wait for the right person. I mean, bike. What if the first time is bad?

Having sex is like riding a bicycle—it's going to make your groin sore.

Having sex is like riding a bicycle—I think I'm ready. He seems like a good person (or bike, whatever) to do it with. I mean, we're friends. I trust him. Am I supposed to wait for some sort of heavenly sign?

Having sex is like riding a bicycle—the first time is scary, but so are a lot of the times after that.

Having sex is like riding a bicycle—you're not supposed to check your phone during it, I learned.

Having sex is like riding a bicycle—you're never really sure you're doing it right.

Having sex is like riding a bicycle—but you can know for sure if the other person's doing it wrong.

Having sex is like riding a bicycle—Scott was actually not a great option. He's a little annoying. Will try Schwinn next time.

Having sex is like riding a bicycle—overrated.

A woman at a party once asked me if I was in a relationship. I said no, and she said, "That's okay!"

I then had to leave the party because my eyeballs were patiently waiting on me to gouge them out. I'll argue until the end of time that we need to let go of the idea that being in a relationship is preferable to being single. It really depends on who you're in a relationship with, what your goals are, how much alone time you like, and what the odds are of having a dramatic meet-cute in a travel bookstore (you'd hate to be in a relationship when Timmy Chalamet walks in).

People toss around so much unsolicited relationship advice. My friend once told me to stop looking for a partner because "it happens when you least expect it." Wait—am I supposed to be tracking how much I expect to fall into a relationship daily over time, so I know when I'm at my low point? How else will I then know it's coming? More to the point—it's impossible to *expect* a relationship anymore, when the definition of a relationship is changing under our very feet. So many of my relationships aren't defined, or they're explicitly casual, or they're on-again-off-again, off-again-off-again, etc. Sometimes I don't find out I was in a relationship until after it's over! Advise me on *that,* Sheila.

I can't tell you whether or not you'll be happy with a committed partner (or what that even means). I can only tell you that based on my own experiences, I can be miserable with just about anyone. I'm no expert—the only thing I know *for sure* about relationships is that calling your romantic partner your "partner in crime" should be more illegal than most actual crimes.

Terms and Conditions for Being My Undefined Partner

1. **Introduction and Acceptance of Agreement:** The following shall define an Undefined Relationship, entered into between me ("Me," "ME") and you ("You," "Hank"). This agreement is a binding contract wherein we can engage in an Undefined Partnership. These terms and conditions contain legal obligations for ensuring the smooth execution of this Undefined Relationship, and it is advisable that you read them closely prior to commitment, as you requested that the following be drawn up when I asked, "What *are* we?" for the nineteenth time.

2. **Official Designation of Relationship:** Our relationship will henceforth be categorized as "Undefined." Alternate terms acceptable for usage on social media or in text messages that either party intends to screenshot for social media include "unlabeled," "thing," and "dating-ish." What we collectively have cannot be defined as a romantic "relationship," but romantic "situation" is fine, as long as the phrase, "but it's not official" always occurs in the same sentence as the term "romantic." Note that this stipulation was yours, not mine.

3. **Ex-Lover Disclosure:** It is advised that you disclose any Undefined or Defined partners from your past, if you have them, which I would prefer you do not. Please also include when you last spoke to them, whether or not you think they're better looking than me, and their Social Security numbers (this is just for my accountant, I don't personally care, although if theirs has more 7s in it than mine, I will be jealous). I'm not legally permitted to get mad at you for speaking with ex-lovers, as this relationship is Undefined, but I am permitted to be vaguely passive-aggressive for several days, should they like one of your Instagrams.

4. **Meeting Important People in My Life:** When you meet friends or anyone with whom I consider myself on amicable terms, you cannot say you're my "friend" as that hurts my feelings, but you also can't say we're "dating," as that will confuse me. You may meet my parents, but only by accident, and only if you're not aware they're my parents. You may not call them by their first names until we've been married five years, should the relationship come to that.

5. **Dispute Resolution Clause:** Should we find ourselves in a dispute—as defined by Me and only Me—the burden of apologizing is on you. This is true regardless of what the fight is, who started it, and whether or not you feel remorse. Because the relationship is Undefined, it does not make logistical sense to work through our issues in a sustainable way, and therefore, an apology on your part should be enough to smooth over any conflict.

6. **TV Shows:** I will pick what we watch until you decide you'd like to make this official. This is a standard clause for all Undefined Relationship agreements, according to my friend who once thought about applying to law school because her floral prints Etsy business was doing poorly. If you'd like to suggest a show, I'd like to suggest a change in relationship status.

7. **Intellectual Property Rights:** I own the right to tweet out anything funny that we say in conversation because I have a bigger following. If something comes up in conversation that I don't intend to use on my Twitter, you may ask my permission to use it on yours, although please be aware that this will make you look pathetic. I will be unlikely to retweet, as our relationship is Undefined. For more frequent retweets, consider changing the designation of this relationship.

8. **Limitation of Liability or Disclaimer:** I don't know what this means. If you'd like this clause removed from the agreement, consider defining the relationship.

9. **Emojis:** Smiley emojis are permissible, but heart-eyes emojis are not allowed. If you'd like to change the status of the relationship, the appropriate emoji is the one with the palms pressed together to indicate "joining." Also, please don't use the grimacing emoji in response to my tweets, as it does have the unintended effect of hurting my little feelings.

10. **Hanging Out When I Don't Feel Like It:** It is permissible that I bail on you should I "not feel like it" at any point. If you take issue with this clause, be advised that you may update the terms and conditions to officially define this relationship.

11. **Notification of Changes:** If at any moment you'd like to be my Defined Partner, let me know. I'm happy to update this agreement immediately, and you will be granted immediate access to my finsta, which I know is what you've wanted all along, you little bitch. Also, if you don't explicitly submit a request to update the relationship, it will automatically roll over into an official relationship within six months. This is an extremely important part of the agreement that I hope you don't read.

12. **Termination:** Please don't.

By clicking the "Agree" button, you give me permission to tell everyone in my life that we are officially Undefined Partners.

AGREE

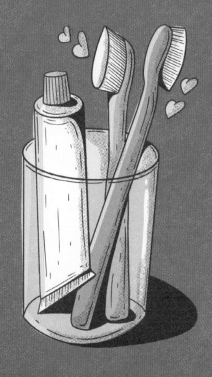

How I Met
Your Father, 2034

Okay, fine. If you really want to know how I met Daddy, I suppose you're old enough to learn. You know how you watched Disney princess movies at Sarah's house? I would never let you, because we're feminists in this household, but I can't control what her mother thinks of *The Little Mermaid* (FWIW, if someone falls in love with you before you've said anything, start screaming). Anyway, in those stories, a beautiful princess is swept off her feet romantically and lovingly by a handsome prince. Well, our love story was . . . a little different.

The year was 2019. Mommy downloaded an app called Hinge. Hinge was basically like Amazon but for single people. You know Amazon, right? The company that controls the world? Well, Mommy was lonely because she'd just been dumped for a much younger woman. A twenty-four-year-old, which might not sound young to you, but it is. Anyone younger than Mommy is objectively very young—always remember that.

Mommy did, once upon a time, have beautiful, long, princess hair, that looked incredible from exactly one angle. And that's the angle from which she photographed it to show to the potential princes on Hinge. When you're old enough, Mommy will help you find your best angle, too. So Mommy started sifting through the princes on Hinge, judging them for who they were as people, nothing else. And then, she saw your daddy.

Daddy's profile was marvelous. He didn't make any jokes—not a single one. No, I know Cookie Monster makes funny jokes, and that's fine; but men, as a general rule, should not. He was also deeply kind, at the time, which Mommy could tell from his photos. Anyway, Mommy swiped right on him, and Daddy swiped right on her back. We were a match! Happily Ever After, algorithm-sent.

One problem, though. This was back in the olden days—I mean, not that old, Mommy's still pretty young—but before our phones were a part of our brains. Sometimes a guy would like you very much and still not check his phone to text you. And that's *definitely* what happened with Daddy.

So Mommy, being the resourceful woman she is—remember how I made a toy out of a cantaloupe rind? It's gross, but I did it—found Daddy on four other dating apps. Maybe he just wasn't checking Hinge specifically, but did really want to meet her, Mommy thought. Maybe he was just testing how hard she was willing to work to go out with him, Mommy thought. Mommy thinks a lot.

Mommy found Daddy on Tinder, which is an app that had to fold in 2026 because it no longer could afford to store 2.8 petabytes of "wyd" messages, but that's neither here nor there. His profile said, "Not looking for anything serious," which Mommy liked, because it meant there was opportunity for a narrative arc in which she could convince him that he was. So Mommy gave Daddy her number. She wasn't about to let him get away.

Four months later, Mommy got a super romantic text from Daddy. It read, "Hey, you gave me your number months ago, want to hang?"

The text came at the perfect time, because it turned out that Mommy *did* want to hang! And she said so. Daddy texted her a few more times to confirm she was the woman he thought she was. She wasn't, but he was open to it anyway. They were off to the races!

Daddy suggested they do the date at his apartment—super romantic, a man who cooks! Daddy rented an apartment with six roommates because he liked to share his toys and toilet paper. He also liked to talk about how he was unwilling to own property in a country that . . . did bad things. Daddy had a lot of opinions about politics. He was really smart.

Mommy and Daddy got along great. They spent the next year . . . hugging. Daddy was hugging other women, too, but he was honest about it, and that's what counts. While Mommy wanted Daddy to hug only her, she appreciated the lack of ambiguity.

Mommy asked her therapist—Oh, what's a therapist? It's someone you're definitely going to need later. Anyway, Mommy asked what it meant when Daddy said he wasn't looking for anything serious, and her therapist kept saying it meant he wasn't looking for anything serious, so Mommy got a new therapist she liked more.

Daddy sort of started texting Mommy less, because he was super busy trying to overthrow the government, which Mommy totally got. She would never want to interfere with him and his Twitter. But a little while later, Mommy met a man who wanted to hug her exclusively, and she moved to Vancouver with him. Mommy thinks Daddy noticed, but she's not sure.

So, Mommy had a lot of opinions about that guy in Vancouver and she doesn't really want to go into all of it, but two years later, he decided to stop hugging Mommy because he needed to "find himself" (sometimes they go missing even though they're in plain sight—this is a weird feature men have, but one that is important for you to know about), so Mommy moved back to San Francisco. She doesn't know whether or not that guy stopped being missing—he didn't have social media. This really annoys Mommy, to this day.

Anyway, that's when things really started to pick up with Daddy. He noticed Mommy's Tinder profile was active again, and he texted her. They resumed hugging. Daddy had grown up a lot—he now had a shower curtain, and he'd become a vegan.

After hugging for years, Mommy and Daddy went on their first date. And their second, and their third. But before their fourth, Daddy decided he and Mommy needed a break so he could hug a few other people. Daddy had this dumb idea that artists gave better hugs, but he got it out of his system. Then he returned to hugging only Mommy.

On their seventh date, Daddy said he wasn't sure he was ready to settle down, but he no longer found the idea as positively terrifying and vomit-inducing as he used to. This brought Mommy a lot of joy. She thought it was very romantic that Daddy didn't think the idea of a future with her would give him diarrhea.

Before their ninth date, Mommy and Daddy spent six hours debating whether or not Mommy could put Daddy in her Instagram story. He said no, but she said she wanted to. Mommy kept asking until finally Daddy said, "Okay, but don't tag me."

Three weeks later, Mommy started tagging Daddy. But despite the tagging, they didn't put a label on it. Mommy didn't know it until she met Daddy, but labels were very bad and toxic to one's health and should be avoided at all costs.

A week after that, Daddy got the flu and needed someone to take care of him, possibly risking getting the flu herself. After that, he decided to put a label on things with Mommy.

A week later, Mommy and Daddy were engaged, but they vowed to not have a wedding because Daddy read a think piece about how weddings are inherently materialistic. Daddy didn't want to make a big deal out of it anyway, I mean, who cares. Mommy cared, but she saw his point about capitalism. Daddy insisted he'd never sign a contract with the state. Daddy was a socialist.

Then a week after that—Oh, what's that? You find this story unromantic? Well, it's not *Ella Enchanted*, but it's not so bad. Do you know how much longer some of Mommy's friends had to hug their partners before they could get a label? A *lot*.

Anyway, then Daddy broke off the engagement to move to Vancouver to find himself. Mommy tried to warn him that, based on her past experience, he probably wasn't there, but he wouldn't listen.

A month after that is when things got a bit juicy. Mommy found out that the pretty little princess ring she put inside her to make sure she could have you . . . at the right time . . . didn't actually work. Also, side note: If those pretty princess rings still sometimes malfunction when you're a grown-up princess, Mommy's gonna flip a shit at how little we care about women's health, but that's neither here nor there. Daddy had always said he thought the ring wasn't inside her anymore, and Mommy thought he was being sooo full of himself for thinking he could "feel it," but turns out it was dislodged. And ineffective.

Daddy had a lot of thoughts about the philosophical underpinnings of bringing human life into this world without its consent—Daddy loved Nietzsche—but overall, Daddy understood that it was Mommy's decision. To bring you into the world . . . a little bit early. Anyway, Daddy thought it was all pretty exciting. He said he thought he'd found himself.

So Mommy moved to Vancouver, again. Mommy's daddy bought Mommy and your daddy a condo, thank God, because neither Mommy nor Daddy could really "afford" things like "that." Daddy, who'd once seemed so opposed to home ownership, was overall pretty happy about it. Maybe because he now lived in Canada. Daddy had always said things were better in Canada, and, honestly, he was right. We lived happily ever after!

New Relationship or Chugging a Cold Brew?

1. Euphoria ♥ OR ☕
2. A general sense of optimism ♥ OR ☕
3. A skip in my step ♥ OR ☕
4. Joy ♥ OR ☕
5. Messy hair ♥ OR ☕
6. An unyielding smile ♥ OR ☕
7. I just got laid. Wooo! ♥ OR ☕
8. Constipated, but in a happy way ♥ OR ☕
9. A belief that I am worthy ♥ OR ☕
10. Confidence that I can accomplish necessary tasks ♥ OR ☕
11. An inability to stop checking my phone ♥ OR ☕
12. More conversations about poop than I had before, but still not as many as I want ♥ OR ☕
13. Extra trips to the bathroom ♥ OR ☕
14. Anxiety attacks, but happy ones ♥ OR ☕
15. Normal anxiety attacks ♥ OR ☕
16. Unpleasant anxiety attacks ♥ OR ☕

17. An elevated heart rate ♥ OR ☕

18. Increased Googling of . . . things ♥ OR ☕

19. Things being my partner's exes ♥ OR ☕

20. What am I hoping to find? I've been ♥ OR ☕
    Googling the same dental student for six
    hours. I found her LinkedIn, and I've looked
    at her parents' house in Alabama from a
    bird's-eye view, but Google isn't going to
    tell me if he still has feelings for her. This is
    a useless endeavor, but one that I've never
    shied away from.

21. Sustained stress about how long this will last ♥ OR ☕

22. A full-blown panic attack ♥ OR ☕

23. A weird brown stain on my white shirt ♥ OR ☕

TEKTUALLY ACTIVE:

Messages I Sent My Tinder Matches the Moment I Started a New Relationship

> Hey! So sorry you never responded to my last 12 messages, it's been crazy over there (I assume). I just wanted to let you know that I met someone, so I'll be deactivating all dating apps. I didn't want to leave you hanging—it was fun getting to know you (in the recesses of my mind).

> Yooooo. I was thinking a lot about that date we went on three years ago. You said you wanted to get drinks again, and though you never reached out, I feel like maybe the offer is still on the table. So I just wanted to clarify that actually, it's not. I have a partner now, and I needed you to know that so you weren't waiting on me for drinks. I hope you find someone wonderful to move on with. xxox

Hey, I saw someone who looked like you at Trader Joe's today, so I figured I'd reach out to let you know I'm now taken. My new partner's really wonderful and definitely acknowledges that they're my partner. Sorry if this message is tough to receive, I just didn't want to leave you hanging.

Heyyyy, Happy Mother's Day to your mom! I am in a relationship now, though, please don't get the wrong idea. I just didn't want to disrespect your mom, whom I've never met.

I think you might have blocked my number so I figured I'd slide into your Instagram DMs. Honesty and transparency are really important to me, and I wanted to let you know that when you said we should "see other people" eight years ago, your advice resonated. I'm now in a relationship, please don't contact me again, even to block me on Instagram too, since that is, in a way, contact, and it's inappropriate, as I'm in a relationship.

Creatively Justify Not Mentioning Your Partner When Sandra Calls You Out

So you've been talking to Sandra for months, and it's been going great. In fact, she seems to like you a lot. There's just one little snafu.

You inconveniently happen to have a partner.

You didn't want to be a buzzkill and bring that up, but unfortunately, Sandra's a bit irritated. Here's how you can calm her down:

- Remind Sandra that you *did* bring up your partner a lot, you just didn't refer to them as your partner. You said "friend," which is also true. The best relationships are built on friendship. Plus, you and your partner *were* friends first, for at least forty-five minutes before you did sex.

- Tell Sandra you never tell anyone you have a partner—they're a Secret.

- Reiterate that there was no reason for you to bring your partner up, because you couldn't possibly imagine that there was any flirty context to you inviting Sandra to stay at your apartment. You specified that you had a couch, after all. I mean, you told Sandra that she could sleep in your bed if she wanted, but you did *mention* the couch.

- Explain that you believe it's rude to mention a partner if not everyone gets one. That's what socialism means to you.

- Clarify that out of respect for your partner's privacy, you keep their identity hidden from women you flirt with. If Sandra had known you had a partner, she might have wanted to know other facts about your partner that could be invasive, like why you never brought her up in the three months of chatting (that's your partner's business, not yours).

- Pretend to be hard of hearing. *Do I have a squirrel friend? No, they scare me.*

- Tell Sandra you were confused—you often forget you have a partner, because you really think of her more as a roommate/sex buddy who also runs errands for you.

- Say that you thought it would be simpler to slowly insult Sandra until she gets the idea that you aren't interested, rather than telling her you're in a relationship. Don't forget that once Sandra begins to think you aren't interested, you must bring it back around and compliment her once, to maintain the friendship and improve the chances she will sleep with you.

- Explain that Sandra's a bit standoffish, so you didn't feel comfortable opening up to her about your personal life. This is also why you haven't responded to her question about whether or not you intend to pay her back for lunch—you're just not comfortable around her.

- "They're not my partner! We're just spouses!"

- Gently, sweetly, softly, repeatedly whisper that Sandra is absolutely insane. This is something women love.

- Tuesday Freebie, we all get one. Today might be Thursday, but Tuesday's right around the corner.

- Divert attention away from it by picking a scab and then bleeding profusely.

- Talk about the weather.

- "What even *is* a partner?"

- Assert that it's actually really hard for you to bring up your partner, because you're tired of being treated differently. You just prefer the way women interact with you when they think you're single. *Not* for flirty reasons, just 'cause.

- Kindly explain that you just wanted a little innocent friendship.

- Kindly explain that you just wanted a little innocent flirting.

- Kindly explain that you just wanted a little innocent sex.

- Fake the death of a close relative to avoid the rest of the conversation.

Present-Day Honeymoon Phases

The term "honeymoon" traditionally refers to the vacation you take after a wedding, so the "honeymoon phase" is the period right after that when the marriage is still fun. However, you may not intend to marry or even DTR with your partner, so I've taken the liberty of providing you with some modern-day honeymoon-phase alternatives.

- The thirty seconds you wait for Tinder to load. You're so full of hope that you're not even mad about the slow Wi-Fi.

- The six hours between matching with them on Tinder and them misspelling "Hey how are you?" as "sup baby i'm thirsty for your mylk."

- The three messages between them asking you out and them suggesting your first date be at their apartment.

- The fifteen minutes on the awkward first date when you get to be eating. This is the most joyful part of any relationship. Order appetizers to stretch it out. At the end of dinner, order dessert. Or more appetizers. There are no rules.

- The hour of excitement after they text you to say they had a great time but before you realize they actually said "good" time. Whatever, you'll take it.

- The month in which they refrain from wearing cargo shorts on dates.

- The four weeks before your friends meet them and realize your descriptors were a bit off. Your new partner doesn't look like Will Arnett. Not even in *BoJack Horseman*.

- The millisecond between when the words "want to read my novel?" leave their mouth and reach your ears.

- The six weeks between making jokes about how crazy you are, and your partner realizing those weren't jokes.

- The four hours you spend discussing how fun it would be to live together, before you get up to pee and are reminded that they don't flush. But, I mean, maybe you can find a two-hundred-square-foot studio apartment with two bathrooms. How hard can it be?

- The twenty-four hours after posting about getting engaged. The "likes" just keep rolling in.

- The month between getting engaged and beginning to research how much weddings cost.

- The part of the wedding when you're eating.

- Also the part of the wedding where everyone talks about how great you are.

- Also the part of the wedding where everyone says you look amazing. You're beginning to understand why people get married so many times.

- Using your vibrator when they're away on business trips. This is the happiest part of any and all marriages.

- The years of marriage in which older relatives stop asking when you plan to get married because you already are, but before close friends start asking when you plan to get divorced.

- The month between agreeing to get divorced and realizing how much divorces cost. It makes no sense—you spend a ton of money getting married. You should get it back (at least for store credit) when you get divorced.

- The first few weeks of divorce when you feel no pressure to date. You breathe a sigh of relief—you've escaped. You won't be one of the 40 percent whose marriage ends in death.

- The thirty seconds you wait for Tinder to load. This time, the slow Wi-Fi annoys you.

Love Songs You'll Realize Are Deeply Unromantic, Once You Think About It One Time

"The Way You Look Tonight" performed by Frank Sinatra: He insists she not change—is she not allowed to age? Get wrinkles? Cellulite? Would that get in the way of her "breathless charm"? Will he even foot the Botox bill? Highly suspicious.

"Beautiful Soul" by Jesse McCartney: This song is three and a half minutes of Jesse McCartney calling his current love interest aesthetically displeasing. Why else would he say he doesn't want a pretty face, but he does want her? No, I am not reading too far into this—this is the only possible interpretation. The point is, Jesse is wrong—nobody wants an ugly face, that's just an indisputable fact.

"What Makes You Beautiful" by One Direction: He literally likes her because she's insecure. If she started going to therapy, would he like her less? Why doesn't he want her to feel good about herself? So many questions.

"Cheerleader" by OMI: I don't condone this relationship, and I literally *was* a cheerleader. Ignoring the obvious misogyny, I don't think this relationship sounds remotely appealing. They don't want someone to challenge them, they just want to be cheered on? If you need constant and unconditional support, call your mom! Also, I wasn't a cheerleader. I just made that up. This is a book, it's called editorializing.

"Stay Stay Stay" by Taylor Swift: This song is catchy (redundant, since it's by Taylor Swift), but in describing her perfect man, she says "You think that it's funny when I'm mad." No! If you think it's funny when I'm mad, then I'm even madder! Take me seriously!

"Escape (The Piña Colada Song)" by Rupert Holmes: Don't even get me started on this one. Don't *even* get me started. The entire premise of the song is that two married people both put out a personal ad to find someone new. And then they find each other, and that's supposed to be cute?! They were both trying to cheat! Wake up, people! Also, he says he never knew that she likes piña coladas. Who doesn't like piña coladas!?

"I Will Follow You into the Dark" by Death Cab for Cutie: I don't know about you, but I don't love it when my partners talk too much about me dying.

"What's My Name?" by Rihanna: I honestly love this song, and I love that there's a math reference, but shouldn't he already know her name?

"Friday I'm in Love" by the Cure: Having dated dozens of people who only show up on the weekend (or whenever), I can assure you that you want a partner who actually does care about you Monday through Thursday.

"Something" by the Beatles: I like that he's trying to be realistic, but he should just go ahead and say his love will grow. He knows that's what she wants to hear—I mean, she literally asked.

"She's Always a Woman" by Billy Joel: Listen to this song again. This woman is a monster. He hates her. You would too.

"She Will Be Loved" by Maroon 5: Get off her corner. That's weird. She doesn't need to know you're following her around—this is a woman who clearly doesn't have a hard time attracting men. Come on.

"Creep" by Radiohead: Actually, this song is extremely romantic. Any song with any connection to *The Social Network* turns me on.

What I Considered Long Distance, by Age

When I was in high school, I thought my boyfriend and I were going to be together forever. I could not fathom there being a better match for me out there, mostly because he was approximately the second non-family-member-boy I'd ever spoken to. And I was willing to go the distance, if that's what it took. However, in the years since, as finding new partners has become swifter with the onset of dating apps, I've become a bit lazier in how far I'll go. While I still see the benefit of a long-distance relationship, my definition has changed. Here's how I'd define it, by age:

Age	*Distance*
18 yrs.	College on different coasts
20 yrs.	Studying abroad in two separate but neighboring European countries
22 yrs.	Having our first jobs in two cities, driving distance apart

24 yrs.	San Francisco to Oakland
26 yrs.	Brooklyn to another part of Brooklyn
28 yrs.	Living in Los Angeles but not in the same apartment. It's a very spread-out city!
29 yrs.	In another room
30 yrs.	On the other end of the couch
32 yrs.	Halfway across the world, if they're nice and don't annoy me. Turns out I was right in high school—it's actually *very* hard to find a good relationship.

The Origin of the Phrase "Partner in Crime"

Abner Jacobs and Beamer Johnson loved each other, but they knew it would never work—their families would never approve. Like Romeo and Juliet or Mark Wahlberg and acting, it was a match doomed to fail.

Twenty-five years before, in the sleepy town of Sleepytown, Beamer's mother reigned supreme as the undefeated chess champion. She'd long been painfully arrogant about her perfect record, and the tiny town itself was painfully cute in how much esteem it gave to its outdoor chess tables. Abner's father had been the second-best chess player for decades, and all he wanted, just once, was to declare victory over her. It was nothing personal; he simply hated women.

And it seemed Abner's father's time had come. He was on the verge of destroying her at last. But just as her clock was running out and his bishop was about to move to check her king, she "pretended" to go into "labor." The game was called off. The next day, Beamer was born. To this day, Abner's father believes it was an excuse—obviously, babies happen when the mothers need them to happen to avoid humiliating defeat. To this day, Beamer's mother resents Abner's father for publicly describing her daughter as a "weak-excuse child." The two families never spoke again.

But their families couldn't stop Abner and Beamer's love. As teens, they'd sneak out of school dances together, sipping water out of flasks (they knew flasks were cool, but no one had told them what to put in them) and touching each other's knees, dramatically, as teens do when they're in love. It was cute. Teens in love are cute in a way that most certainly disgusts any viewer.

In college, they continued a long-distance correspondence while enjoying their own Franzia-addled adventures with lanky frat boys—none lanky enough to take the other's place. They'd return home for the holidays and sneak out after their parents had drifted off into an eggnog-induced slumber. They'd reunite in the back of Beamer's car, finally having figured out what to put in flasks (lubricant). Their love did not wane.

After college, both moved home, because the alternative was getting jobs, and who has the time for that? Besides, Abner worried his Good Charlotte posters would rip if he tore them off the wall of his childhood bedroom; he couldn't risk it.

There was just one problem—their love still had to be secret. In fact, Beamer's mother woke Beamer up every morning with a reminder that the Jacobses were actually the ones who started the flat-earth theory, and anyone who spreads rumors like that is evil. And Abner's father, as he sat reading *Playboy* and the newspaper every morning, would remind Abner to spit on Beamer's lawn, should he pass it. And so, Abner and Beamer were stuck having sex in each other's cars.

Abner was in pain. He was simply too tall for the back seat of Beamer's car. Sex in the back seat of a car was gross-cute in high school, but now it was just plain uncomfortable.

"This car thing isn't working anymore," Abner said one night. It was 10 p.m., and Sleepytown was sleepy. They were on the golf course—their favorite spot to park and play. Abner always thought golf was a lot like sex, in that he was bad at both. "We need another place to have sex."

"We could get jobs," Beamer suggested. "And then our own apartments."

Abner rolled down the windows, frustrated. Beamer didn't get it. Things kept him at his parents' house. *Important* things. Like, his Good Charlotte posters. What if they ripped? You can't just buy new ones—that's humiliating. Abner opened the door to get some air.

Just then, a golf ball went whizzing past them. At 10 p.m.? Who was playing right now? It's called Sleepytown, not Late-Night-Golftown. That's two towns over.

Beamer heard a clunk, and then a scream. Abner stepped out of the car.

"AaAAbCDDEfffGHiJJJJJ!" Another scream, somehow impressively alphabetized. It seemed that the ball had hit somebody. And that whoever got hit was *not* happy about it.

Abner and Beamer headed in the direction of the noise. Another scream, behind a tree. A man lay there, still.

"Hey," said Beamer. "Are you okay?"

Silence.

"If you're dead, let us know so we can call someone," said Abner.

Silence.

"I think he's dead," said Beamer.

"But wouldn't he have told us that?" Abner asked.

The two were confused and scared. It was one thing to carry on a secret romance for ten years. But a death? That was a *second* thing. For two twenty-five-year-olds who weren't yet ready to enter the workforce, that was one thing too many. Sure, the media makes it look adorable when lovers hide a death together, but it was surely just another phenomenon that became gross once you leaned too far into it. They got back into Beamer's car and drove home.

The death on the golf course dominated town discourse for the next several weeks. No one knew who'd killed him, and *everyone* seemed to have an alibi. Yes, every single resident of Sleepytown went to bed before 10 p.m. It's almost as if they should have called the town Sleepyt— Oh, wait. But, anyway, everyone had indeed been asleep, and they could prove it by showing the event on their phone that said, "9:45 p.m.— bedtime." It was a rock-solid, unquestionable alibi—Kavanaugh-style.

Everyone, except Abner and Beamer.

The pair tried to lay low, but it wasn't long before the investigator, Cadmire, had started asking about them. It was a small town. And people don't just *leave their towns* to kill someone—the murderer was a Sleepytown resident. And Cadmire had interviewed just about everyone else. Everyone had said they'd been asleep. People who were asleep couldn't murder someone, and people who were awake wouldn't say they were asleep. Obviously.

Six days after the murder, Cadmire knocked on Beamer's door. Her mother answered, in a bathrobe. She had been fully clothed but changed into a robe the moment she heard a knock on the door. Beamer's father had left her years ago to die, and she was Lonely.

"How can I help you?" she asked. Cadmire wasn't good-looking, but he was a man. She put her finger in her mouth. "I'm really good at chess."

"As you know, we're investigating a murder. I need to take your daughter in for questioning," said Cadmire.

"Sure, no problem," said Beamer's mom.

"It'll just be her and Abner Jacobs. They're the only two suspects left. We think they may have been in cahoots."

Beamer's mom went pale. "Don't you come around here making accusations like that!" she said, sticking her finger in his face. "My Beamer may have killed a man, but she didn't do it with a *Jacobs,* I can guarantee it. We don't go near that family, that much I promise you."

"How do you know?"

"Because Beamer hasn't told me she's started dating at all. We're super close—she'll tell me when she wants to start, just like she'll tell me when she first gets her period, probably any day now."

Cadmire shrugged. "We'll figure it out when we bring her in for questioning."

Right before their questioning, Abner and Beamer shared a private moment together. "Are you nervous?" Abner asked.

"A little," Beamer confessed. "I don't want to say the wrong thing."

"Just don't say we were together," said Abner. "Our families will never forgive us."

"Right, and don't say we killed him," said Beamer.

"Why not?"

"Because we didn't. And doing so will get us sent to jail. Plus, killing people is gross, and we don't want to be gross."

"Oh, right."

Cadmire came in to get them. He didn't appear nervous—it was his job to look mean, as for most members of law enforcement. He wanted to intimidate people into confessing to things, regardless of what those things were. Cadmire had loved confessions ever since he watched *Confessions of a Teenage Drama Queen* as a young boy. But it was more than that—Cadmire had a secret.

You see, Cadmire may have lived two towns over, in the town of Late-Night-Golf-town. But his favorite nighttime golf spot—well, that was in Sleepytown. And one week ago, he'd found himself there at around 10 p.m. and—you guessed it. Yes, it was an accident. But it *was* Cadmire.

If he couldn't find a way to pin this on Abner and Beamer, well then, he was done for. Metaphorically, that is. The investigation was never going to turn on him, since he was the one running it, but he figured he might as well be on the safe side and send two innocent kids to jail.

Thus far, Abner and Beamer maintained that they hadn't been together that night. And this defense seemed suitable—to kill someone with a golf ball, the jury believed, you needed at least two people swinging on the stick. Cadmire knew better, but if he wanted to get the jury on his side, he had to prove they were in the same place.

The questioning began.

"Where were you the night of June 10, 2014?"

"On the street," said Abner.

"What street?"

"I can't remember."

"That's convenient."

Beamer burrowed her head in her arms. They'd spent so much time preparing for the questioning, but they hadn't thought to cover that one. Shoot.

"What about you, Beamer?"

"I went out for a walk around 9:45, to get some fresh air. I live on Dover Street, and I turned left onto Orchard to walk, for about fifteen minutes."

"On Orchard, you say?" asked Cadmire.

"Yes . . . Orchard," Beamer answered nervously.

"Where Abner lives?"

Beamer swallowed. Abner did, in fact, live on Orchard. She didn't mean to name Abner's street, she just couldn't think of any others. What was Cadmire getting at?

"So you mean to tell me you went for a walk on Abner's street, and Abner was out-side on some *unnamed* street, and the two of you are the *only* people in town without alibis? It seems awfully suspicious—you were on the street, she was on the street, it was nighttime, a man died on a golf course. There aren't that many streets. Help me understand—were you on the street together?"

"No, Beamer and I weren't together on the street," said Abner. "We couldn't have killed the man. We were in a car. I mean—"

That was it. He'd done them in. Beamer's eyes darted to her mother, who had come to the police station for fun, as it was a *very* sleepy town. She burst into tears. How could Beamer have done this to her? Beamer's heart broke. She had to do some-thing—nothing was worse than the disappointment in her mother's eyes.

"Aha! And what were you doing in a car together?" asked Cadmire.

"It's not because of anything suspicious, it's just because we're partners—" Abner began.

"In crime!" Beamer yelled. "In crime. We killed him together, because we're part-ners in crime. Abner, here, he's my partner in crime. But on a personal level, we hate each other and would *never* date."

Beamer's mother's tears dried instantly, like something out of a Bounty commer-cial. Abner's parents joyfully high-fived. Cadmire was the most victorious of all.

"To jail it is!" he said. "A lifetime for both of them, for these two Partners in Crime!"

And so, Abner and Beamer got to spend a life together in the same jail cell, because that's what happened to Partners in Crime. Those who commit together, serve together. The pair could not have been more stoked. Finally, they found a way out of their parents' houses. And they didn't have to hide their love anymore, they could live together in peace.

The two of them were marched toward the jail. When they thought no one was looking, Abner sneaked a kiss. "So happy to have you as my Partner in Crime," he said. Beamer giggled, ashamed. Sure, the phrase was cute and funny because it ref-erenced an event that had just happened, but it was also gross. She'd let Abner say it exactly one time, and then she'd clamp down on that sort of inappropriate display of affection.

The only witness who overheard Abner was a preteen girl with a smartphone—the most lethal kind. The preteen girl took a liking to the phrase, and vowed that as soon as she got a boyfriend, she would refer to him as her Partner in Crime. Ah, if only that girl had never found a mate. If only, if only. But most origin stories are tales of misfortune, like Wolverine or whatever. Batman. The polio vaccine.

And then, as the guard locked the gate on them, sentencing them to a life of love and passion, Beamer pulled out her Instagram. She snapped a photo of Abner. "Stuck with this one," she captioned it. And she meant it literally—the door was locked, they'd never be free. If she'd only known what sort of trend she was starting . . . how many engagement photos would bear the same caption . . . she never would have forgiven herself. Because starting a gross trend like that—well, that's the real crime.

The Point of Holding Hands in Public

- To not get lost in crowds

- To initiate a game of Red Rover

- To share sweat, so your sweats don't get lonely

- To show people you're so happy with your partner you don't mind overheating your hands just for the sake of showing affection

- To spend some time away from your phone, or at least slow down your phone usage by only having one hand available

- To compare nail polish colors

- To keep your fingers from falling off (I don't know your life!)

- To take advantage of the advanced functionality of the human fingers. We're the only species that can hold hands—did you know that? It's not true, but you believed it for a second, didn't you?

- To act out the Hush Sound song, "We Intertwined." It's catchy!

- To prevent your partner from describing you as their "friend" should they run into an ex

- Because feet don't clasp together that easily

- To make a point, I guess. That you're in a relationship, I assume. Nice.

Choose the Right Show to Binge-Watch at Every Stage of a Relationship

Being in a long-term relationship is mostly just saying, "We should watch that together" about a show exactly one of you enjoyed exactly eight years ago. However, *that show* is an ambiguous term, because there is a different correct show for each stage in a relationship.

First Five Dates: Fun fact: Half of all conversations before a couple is officially dating begin with, "Did you see that tweet?" If you're going to watch a show together on the first few dates, choose the most overhyped one of the day, for the sake of conversation. This opens the door to sending each other *Atlantic* articles about it afterward, which is helpful (to rule out the type of person who does this).

Unofficially Dating: You need to be careful not to scare each other in the early stages. Watch the least sexy/romantic show you can, to make sure you both stay calm—a character expressing feelings to another on-screen could cause your relationship to begin to feel rushed. May I suggest *Tiger King* or *The Simpsons*?

Honeymoon Phase: You're still in a place where you're willing to accommodate each other's interests. In my experience, this is usually when I watch *Sports* on ESPN. You don't need to have seen the earlier seasons to follow.

In Anticipation of Meeting the Parents: Find out their political affiliation first, and then watch *Real Time with Bill Maher* regardless of what it is. Parents love two things—discussing minor and seemingly insignificant differences between their children, and this show.

During Sex: This is an entire stage of a relationship, and the only two options are porn and infomercials. You must be either fully engaged or not at all.

Boring Middle: You're finally ready to give your full attention to a TV show, so I'd suggest *Game of Thrones or* any other HBO drama. You don't want to start an eleven-season prestige drama until you know you're ready to settle down for a minute, because *The Wire* isn't something you can just get out of.

After Saying "I Love You": *Curb Your Enthusiasm,* to balance out any IRL sap. You don't want to walk around just feeling good about things.

Taking a Three-Month Break: Unfortunately, after watching enough Larry David, you were actually cured of loving each other. During this break, forgo the TV in favor of reading a book. Or take a vacation to Canada—the only chance you'll ever have to find yourself.

Getting Back Together: *Curb Your Enthusiasm* again, because you were really enjoying it before the two of you broke up. But limit it to one season this time; you know the risks.

Moving in Together: Rachael Ray, Kardea Brown, or anyone else on the Food Network. It's time to domesticate.

The Two Months of Prolonged Conversation About Whether or Not to Break Up: Something animated—it's time to escape reality.

Post Breakup: *Curb Your Enthusiasm,* again. It's a funny show.

This list is just a suggestion. You can watch whatever you want, but there's one hard-and-fast rule—if your partner has seen *The Office* and you haven't, you canno*t ever* watch it, at least not until you've broken up. I promise you, every joke your partner has ever made was probably ripped off from this show. It will ruin them for you.

Fighting is as natural as clipping your toenails, in that I only do it when I'm dating someone. I've had several profound realizations in my years of fighting with partners. The first was to not fight via text. The second was to ask myself if I was hungry, before picking a fight. The third, and most unfortunate, was that I initiated approximately 92 percent of romantic fights I've been in. I don't think fights are necessarily unhealthy, but my goal for my next relationship is to get that number down to about 91 percent.

Along the way, I learned how to fight (use *I* statements, like "*I* think you're an idiot"), how to stay calm when I'm upset (take deep breaths and refresh every app on my phone), and how to forgive (put yourself in their shoes, even if your partner wears Crocs). Some fights were so obviously foreboding of a great incompatibility that I can't believe we tried to stay together afterward. But some fights were so funny that it's all I can do not to look back in laughter.

Quiz

Line from a Tampon Commercial, or Me and My Ex Trying to Buy a Deformed Rotisserie Chicken and Then Slowly Devolving into Fighting About Our Overall Compatibility?

1. I know what you're thinking—this thing looks huge.

2. You have to change it every three hours, so get something manageable.

3. You don't know how you'll like it until you try.

4. There are going to be clumps, but they can always be hidden.

5. Why are there holes?

6. Go down a size.

7. $24 just seems like too much.

8. A five-ingredient formula you can trust.

9. Actually, we *can* stop the leaking.

10. Is something stuck up there?

11. That's 7x more than you may need.

12. The red patch of courage!

13. Why are you so scared to be adventurous?

14. You barely feel anything.

15. I know you're upset because I know your cycle.

16.   Oh, I see. It's the general discomfort you exist with, every single day.

17.   Are you ashamed of who you are?

18.   It's time to stop worrying about what's in your pants.

19.   No *wonder* more women trust Always.

20.   Show me what it looks like to fight like a girl.

21.   You're so insecure, I can't handle it. It's like my role in the relationship is to validate you, and it just gets exhausting after a while.

22.   It's probably inedible.

23.   You *always* get to pick the chicken. It's like, do you even see me? Do I have a role in this relationship? Or will we just spend the rest of our days arguing over chickens, because you're not willing to take a chance and try the Huli Huli recipe, just this once?

24.   And then you take all these negative feelings, and instead of going to a therapist like I always suggest, you take it out on me. Let's just get a pizza. This isn't worth it.

25.   It's like, you barely feel *anything*.

26.   Do you have *any* emotions?

27.   Max.

28.   *Max.*

29.   Some people simply can't handle the truth.

30.   Oh, you think I *want* to fight? No, Max, I don't *want* to, you just push me to the point where I have to. And besides, you said you didn't even consider something a fight unless both parties were mad, by which definition, I've never gotten in a fight with a romantic partner in my life.

31.   I'm not mad, I'm just menstruating.

32.   Sorry.

33.   This relationship is too much for me.

34.   Sorry.

35.   Okay, I'm telling my parents you can't make it to dinner. And I'm getting tacos for them—you know I hate cooking, but you always pushed me on the rotisserie chicken. You tried to turn me into someone I wasn't at every step in this relationship. Like the time you left a toothbrush at my house. Maybe I wasn't meant to be a person who brushed their teeth! Why can't you just accept me?!

36.   Good-bye forever, Max.

37.   Produces 60 percent less waste than traditional period products. The only tampon with 360° protection.

Answers:

1–37: It's impossible to tell.

What My Therapist Recommends I Say in a Fight vs. What I Say in a Fight

My partner is mad I'm late.

What my therapist recommends: I understand you're upset. I wasn't demonstrating that I valued your time, and that's not right. I also think it's possible I triggered your fears of abandonment from childhood, and your reaction could potentially be a projection, but I want us to work together to ensure that you feel confident in this relationship.

What I said: I'm not late, you're early.

My partner is upset my apartment is messy.

What my therapist recommends: You're right. I should tidy up to foster a comfortable and stress-free environment for both you and myself.

What I said: This isn't your royal castle. If you don't respect the way I live, this will never work.

My partner is pushing me to spend too much time with their family.

What my therapist recommends: I really appreciate that you're bringing me into your life, but I have responsibilities of my own, so I'd like to keep the dinners with your parents to once a month for right now. It's not that I don't like them, it's just that I don't want to rush into things too quickly.

What I said: Your mom's a lot, and I'm not the only one who thinks that. Mmmmm-kay?

My partner's mother is putting a lot of pressure on me to have kids.

What my therapist recommends: You're concerned about your bloodline and who will take charge of the family business, and I understand that. Still, this is something he and I would like to discuss separately, so it'd be much appreciated if you didn't tell reporters that I'm soon-to-be carrying the heir to the throne.

What I said: Pry my IUD out of my cold, wet vagina. Or, if we're being honest, dry vagina.

I don't like being hounded by paparazzi.

What my therapist recommends: Hey, could we maybe get a place somewhere a little more remote? I'm just a private person, and having the paparazzi around makes me feel anxious.

What I said: If you don't get rid of them, I will walk outside nude. How would the Queen like *that*?

We can't agree on a theme for a wedding.

What my therapist recommends: I know tradition is important to you. Maybe we can find some middle ground where I can respect your family history while also not wearing white, because I could menstruate at any moment. Like, *any* moment.

What I said: I don't *want* a royal wedding! I want it to be *Buffy the Vampire Slayer*–themed; I've been saying this from the first day we ever met. Do you not remember? You were like, "Don't bring up your wedding, we just met."

My partner wants me to give up my career to fulfill my duties as a royal.

What my therapist recommends: As you know, my career is very important to me. This has always been true, even though I did quit my job three months ago to focus on my lifestyle blog (I told you, I'll do the first post once my homemade kefir successfully curdles), but still. I think we can find a way for me to attend formal family balls and use your parents' private island without me compromising what I've worked for.

What I said: No offense to your family, but being a royal is not a "job."

My partner doesn't understand why I feel trapped.

What my therapist recommends: I feel trapped when you tell me the only thing I'm ever going to be is a princess or queen, and that I'm your country's last hope. If you guys would be willing to compromise on the patriarchy thing, maybe your sister could rule? She's way more adult than I am. Like, she puts ice cream in bowls before eating it.

What I said: This is *not* what the Disney Channel said it would be.

I'm not getting the attention I need from my partner, so I'm acting out.

What my therapist recommends: I recognize where you're coming from. You told me from the day we met that if this were to get serious, I'd have to be a professional royal. I'm sorry I smashed your dad's 800-year-old plate that apparently some king gave him, and I shouldn't have done that. I also definitely shouldn't have done that while yelling about how Anne Hathaway never would have stood for this shit in *The Princess Diaries*. I'm sorry again, and upon further reflection, yes, she would have stood for it. She had no spine. She couldn't even admit to her best friend she straightened her hair.

What I said: Look, the king whose plates I smashed was probably really racist 800 years ago.

Okay, yeah, I probably shouldn't have stolen the crown jewels.

What my therapist recommends: I was feeling stressed out about my responsibilities, and I resorted to an unhealthy coping mechanism. I understand that my actions made you feel like you can't trust me anymore, and I'm sorry.

What I said: Lol, crown jewels. Like, penis.

But do I deserve to be beheaded?

What my therapist recommends: Hey, I know things didn't go as planned, but I really value the connection we had, and I think we should try to remember the good times before we jump to swift action.

What I said: Fuck, are you serious? They can't still do that—where is the United Nations!? Doesn't the Geneva Convention outlaw this sort of thing!? If you don't let me out of this dungeon, I'm gonna blow you guys up on Twitter, you'll be sorry! Dammit! There's no service down here!!!

My partner has dumped me and now blocked me on Instagram.

What my therapist recommends: Thank you for communicating your needs. It's probably better if I don't IG-stalk you anyway, so we can both move on.

What I said: Sucks to suck, I set a Google alert for your name, Prince Doofus. And I'll keep stalking you until the moment they chop off my h—

Keep It Under Control When Your New Partner Turns Out to Be a Broomstick in a Trench Coat

It happens to all of us—a new relationship feels off to a good start, you're getting to know each other, the sex is amazing. Then, all of a sudden, without warning, it takes a turn for the worse. One night, while they're sleeping, you look over at them. Wait—you can't hear them breathing. Hold on a second. That's . . . that's not a person. That's a broomstick in a trench coat. What do you do?

Stay calm. It's obviously jarring to learn your partner is not who you thought they were. I once was dating a super nice woman, only later to learn that every Monday night, she played Magic: The Gathering with her friends until 4 a.m. and had *never once won*. If your partner isn't who you believed them to be, take a deep breath before expressing anger. If you let your fury get the better of you, you might end up snapping your partner in half.

Give them a chance to explain themselves. Everyone deserves to be heard. You've had some good times with your broomstick in a trench coat—remember when they took you to see *Naked Gun* at the drive-through? In retrospect, the fact that they didn't laugh should have been a clue, but you just figured they had a sophisticated sense of humor. Still, you owe it to them to listen—maybe there's a solid explanation for why they've been deceiving you this whole time.

Stay safe. If you've been sleeping with a broomstick in a trench coat for the last six months, you're at low risk for STDs and pregnancy. However, low doesn't mean zero, and besides, you can get a mean yeast infection, depending on which end you— Never mind.

Be forgiving. You might not realize how hard it is for broomsticks in trench coats to find love. Often, they're stored in a closet entirely alone, or with just one other broom. Think about how annoying it is when your friends assume you want to be set up with their only other single friend—you can have exactly one option and still be lonely.

Ask yourself if the problem might be you. Did you ever explicitly say you yourself *weren't* a broomstick in a trench coat? That's a bit human-normalizing, isn't it? And why are you so desperate to hold their hand—are you needy? You got on for years without holding anyone's hand, so it feels a bit pushy to insist the broomstick grab onto you now. Especially because you know it can't.

Wonder what role society plays in your preconceived disdain for dating a broomstick in a trench coat. The idea that we can't date broomsticks was clearly put in our heads by the media. Maybe if Rory had just *once* dated a broomstick in a trench coat, we'd be a little more forgiving (and she maybe wouldn't have dated Logan, ugh).

Think about the positives. You know how all your straight female friends complain about their partners losing their erections? That's not really on your radar. Besides, how many times has a human person stomped all over your heart? Ghosted you? Told you your makeup made you look like a bat? Your broomstick in a trench coat did *none* of those things, and it's never *once* mansplained.

Clean your floor. Dating a broomstick in a trench coat while having dirty floors would be like dating a photographer but still having to pay for your own nudes. Take advantage of the perks!

Start looking up the price of cute dustpans. Their birthday might be right around the corner.

Embrace your new life. Welcome to the new you, sparkly floors and all. It's time to start holding their handle instead, and accept that you love who you love.

Benefits of My Partner Saying Exactly What I Want to Hear, Instead of Me Saying It to Myself

Hey, you've brought up a really great point. Sometimes, when we're fighting, it feels like there's exactly one thing I want to hear, and I'm not satisfied until you say it. This is true, but I'd just like to point out that this isn't restricted to when we're fighting—I actually *always* want you to say exactly what I want to hear, and I think it's a bit inconsiderate when you don't accommodate this.

But *you* seem erroneously to think that this is some sort of issue. Of course, I want you to say exactly what I want to hear—why would anyone ever not want that? It's literally a tautology. And yet, you've gone so far as to suggest that if there's just one thing I want to hear, I should just say it to myself. Like, if I want to know if I'm being irrational, and the only acceptable answer is yes, I should just look in the mirror and tell myself that. I obviously can't do that. That would make me look *insane*. Which I'm not. I'm rational, thanks for reminding me of this fact.

I know you think you're generally useless, and I totally get why you feel that way (for starters, you are). However, that doesn't mean I don't prefer hearing the words come out of your mouth rather than having to say them myself. Do you know that expression "straight from the horse's mouth"? That was about a lady horse who asked her partner if her saddle made her look fat. I want to hear it from you. I can't say it to myself. I *need* to hear it from you.

Why do I need to *hear* you say that you're happier with me than with your ex? I don't know, maybe because I had a tumultuous childhood in which I watched a little too much *Grey's Anatomy* and saw firsthand Derek leave Meredith for Addison. And that's really not a me-thing. It's a you-thing. Fix it, by saying exactly what I want to hear. Plus, when you go back on what you said later on, I have something concrete to be mad about. Another benefit of you saying it, not me.

I'm not doing this for me. I'm doing this for us. Kind of like why I always pee after sex. *We* don't want UTIs.

Finally, I'd just like to say that it's completely normal of me to want this. And that's what I expect you to say back to me, when I ask if it's completely normal of me to want this. Please and thank you.

Quiz

What Are You Really Fighting About?

If you're anything like me, you're in a fight with your partner right now. However, the fights are almost never about what you initially think they're about. Take this quiz to find out what's *actually* causing the rift.

1. Your partner tells you you're driving too fast. Are you fighting about:

a. Your driving

b. The fact that you pressured them into living in Los Angeles when they much preferred Chicago, a city with good public transit and easy access to their ailing parents

2. Your partner is mad you spent $40 on a new towel. Are you fighting about:

a. The cost of the towel

b. Spending $40 without asking them, even though they're currently the only one making an income

3. There are stacks of dirty dishes in the fridge. Are you fighting about:

a. The fruit flies

b. The fact that you can't be bothered to do the dishes even though you haven't booked an audition in over a month. It's like, you made your partner move here, just for you to not even pursue your dreams, but on top of that, you're too depressed to take care of the apartment—which you can't afford to live in without them. This is *not* what *La La Land* said it would be like. Not for you, not for your partner, not even for that guy who spilled coffee on Emma Stone. It was the last time he made three figures to spill *anything*.

4. Your partner never replaces the last roll of toilet paper. Are you fighting about:

a. Shared responsibility for the apartment

b. The word "roll" is actually really triggering for you because it's a homophone for "role," which you're not getting

5. You can't decide how many times a week to have sex. Are you fighting about:

a. Your libidos

b. Your partner's inability to understand that you just don't *feel* sexy when your agent's said you don't look young enough to play high school anymore. Being 35 is brutal. You don't know how the gals from *Sex and the City* did it.

6. Your partner won yet another game of Scrabble. Are you fighting about:

a. How the same person always wins Scrabble, no matter who's playing. This game is rigged.

b. How you need to get creative with your career if you ever want to get *anyone's* attention, but how can you do that when you're not even creative enough to realize that "zestiets" can be rearranged to spell "zestiest"

7. You want to stay in on a Saturday night, but your partner insists you go to her coworker's party. Are you fighting about:

a. How lazy you are

b. How you just got a new podcast idea, and even though it's Saturday night and you haven't had a regular job in months, so you technically have all the time in the world to start it, you absolutely must capitalize on your burst of creativity and do it right this instant! Who knows—if you go out tonight, someone younger and hotter than you might start the podcast first. And podcasts are the new way to fame. I mean, even Hillary Clinton has one.

8. You don't know if you want to raise your kids religiously or not. Are you fighting about:

a. Religion, which has never mattered much to either of you

b. Your unborn children

c. The fact that you now have an audience of over 500 listeners per week who find the drama in your relationship "funny" and enjoy when you do an impression of your partner explaining the genius of David Lynch for 45 minutes, during which time you actually learned a lot (mostly about your partner, but still).

9. Your partner comments that it's raining. Are you fighting about:

a. Nothing, this isn't a fight

b. How they don't respect you or your newfound success, not even the tiniest bit. You're more than just a voice of our generation. As a podcast host, you provide the most valuable service available—you remind subscribers what day of the week it is. And you *matter*.

10. Your partner takes over an hour in the bathroom every morning. Are you fighting about:

a. The one shared toilet

b. Them trying to hide from you in your own home because you now use your whole relationship as content, including but not limited to their personal grooming habits and familial relationships. The listeners love it! Your partner, unfortunately, does not. Good news, though—they're now your ex-partner.

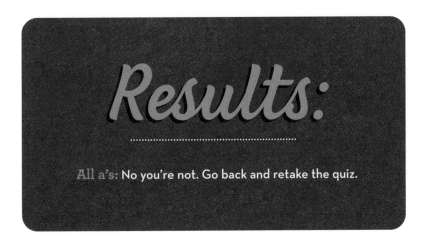

Results:

All a's: No you're not. Go back and retake the quiz.

Marry/Fuck/Kills for the Person Who's Been Dating for Too Long

The game marry/fuck/kill is fun and simple. Out of three people, you must instantly decide whom you want to spend the rest of your life with, whom you're lukewarm about (and will therefore sleep with), and whom you want dead. I've never fully understood the game because I've never slept with anyone I did not, at some point, want to kill, but I see the appeal. After dating for so many years, I've come up with a few real stumpers. Get ready to spend some time thinking.

....

The Tinder user who immediately sends a dick pic

The Tinder user who reels you in with "What's up?" and then sends a dick pic

The Tinder user who opens with "Happy Monday!"
....

The person who misspells "Hey" ("Hay")

The person who misspells "sup" ("supp")

The person who misspells your name
....

The OkCupid-er who sends you a copy-pasted 200-word message

The OkCupid-er who only speaks in one-word answers

The OkCupid-er who uses more emojis than words

....

The lady who watches your Instagram story within the
first five minutes of you posting it

The lady who looks up your LinkedIn every day

The lady who didn't bother to Google you at all

Your Wi-Fi-powered vibrator

Your battery-operated vibrator

Your hand

The woman who texts constantly but won't make plans

The woman who's super attentive IRL but takes hours to text back

The woman who thinks it's okay to use FaceTime without warning

The man who calls you the wrong name during sex

The man who calls you "pushy" for asking if you can take things slow

The man who doesn't call you at all

The 32-year-old who says they're not looking for anything serious

The 38-year-old who says they're too young to settle down

The 23-year-old who says they "love older women" (you're 27)

The dude who takes three months to give you their Wi-Fi password

The dude who takes five months to commit to being in a relationship

The dude who takes seven months to learn to put the toilet seat down

Your sexual partner who doesn't talk to their mom

Your sexual partner who talks to their mom for two hours every day

Your sexual partner who treats you like their mom

The guy with a super-clean apartment who won't lend you his Roomba

The guy with the dirty apartment whose dick is
the length of a broomstick

Henry the Fruit Fly, who basically does the cleaning

The person with six roommates but also six
streaming service accounts

The person who has their own apartment but no Netflix

The person who lives two hours away but really, truly loves you

The loser who ghosts after two dates

The loser who dramatically breaks up with you before you've met IRL

The loser who dates you for years, tells you you're the love of
their life, talks about a future together, and then one day, without
warning, decides it's not working out

The guy who leaves the toilet seat up

The guy who leaves dirty dishes in the sink

The guy who leaves you

Grubhub

Uber Eats

Postmates

10 Things I Just Realized
I Hate About You

I hate the way you talk to me
I hate your creepy stare

I hate it that you don't live far
I hate your ego and your thinning hair

I hate your big, dumb, stupid thoughts
And the way you question mine

You think you're smart, it makes me sick
It even makes me rhyme

I hate the way you're never right
Like, to the point where you shouldn't even try

I hate that you can't make me laugh
Your jokes—they make me cry

I hate it when you *are* around
And the fact that you sometimes call

Actually, I totally just hate you
I'm not sure I even ever liked you
Not even close
Not even a little bit
Not even at all

Not to brag, but I have a *lot* of experience with getting dumped. I once got dumped immediately post-coitus by a close friend. I once got dumped while trying to ghost someone. I once got dumped in the Quiznos in the food court of a Westfield mall on my twenty-second birthday. (I never enjoyed their sandwiches again, although, to be fair, I hadn't ever enjoyed them before.) I even got dumped at work (or, as my mother likes to call it, "fired"). I've been dumped a lot!

Getting dumped is one of the worst things that can happen in a relationship, perhaps second only to having to dump someone. Actually, maybe staying in a bad relationship is the worst. I also don't like the part of a relationship when they run out of peanut butter. I don't know—relationships have so many risks.

With breakups come exes, although, not to brag *again*, but I don't need to have dated someone to consider them an "ex" (broken eye contact is usually enough). I'm on fine terms with a lot of my exes, as I don't hold grudges (I just choose to permanently like people slightly less). In fact, I cherish some of my exes, mostly because I still use their Hulu logins. Plus, as my therapist always says, you only get dumped if someone wanted to date you in the first place. So let's change the narrative—breakups don't have to be romantic defeats, and your exes don't have to be antagonists. Because, I promise you, every single one of them is still thinking about you.

Suitable Responses to "We Should See Other People"

You've been dumped—it happens to the best of us (not everyone, just the best of us). And—you guessed it—your ex told you that you should "see other people." If you need to respond to this unsatisfying breakup line, feel free to use one of these.

- Actually, I think we should both separately be alone.

- Did you just break up with me and then give me instructions on what to do next?

- Agreed. We should probably start phone banking for our local city councilperson, too, while we're on the subject of self-improvement.

- Any recommendations?

- Lol.

- I have eyeballs, I already see other people.

- In that case, is your friend Harry single?

- Your sister? Is she still married?

- No thanks, you've turned me off of dating forever.

- I'm melting!!

- Your Uncle Jeff? I found him on Instagram, could you introduce us?

- I'm actually going to see the same person, over and over again.

- Okay, in that case, I'm keeping the Roomba.

End Any Type of Relationship

Dating terms today are nebulous. For example, I hang out with this guy at least every other month, he takes six hours to respond to my texts, and he's told me fifteen times that he's not my boyfriend; so, is he my boyfriend? With all this understandable confusion, it can be hard to figure out not only what to call someone you're dating but also how to call it quits. I created this handy guide to help you out.

Hanging Out: If you've been "hanging out with" someone, you may decide the time has come to "hang out with other people." Do this via text—a phone call would be way too much commitment.

Hooking Up: If you've been "hooking up" with someone and you want to "unhook" yourself, your best bet is to say your dog is sick every time they ask you to hang out, and keep this up for the next six years. They may ask if it's time to consider putting the dog down, but that's really not your problem—you don't even have a dog.

Texting: It's inappropriate to use a text to dump someone you've been texting with. That's like ruining your special thing. Instead, do it in person, even if it's the only time the two of you have ever met.

Seeing Each Other: If you've been "seeing each other" and you want to stop, simply say that you've disliked what you've seen so far. Everyone gets it. They won't take it personally—it's just aesthetics.

Sleeping Together: This one is self-explanatory—just wake up.

Talking: Somehow, "talking" is more serious than sleeping together, and if you're talking to someone and want to break up, just trying shutting your mouth. No one wants to talk to someone who can't talk.

Going Steady: I guess send a telegram back to 1955?

In a Relationship: I don't have experience with this one. Pass.

Breadcrumbing: I think this one is a bad thing but I'm not sure. Remind them that you're gluten-free—that should solve the problem.

Jibing: This is like "vibing" for people who meet on Sea Captain Date. You can get out of this situation by jumping overboard—hope you brought a life vest!

Burning: I don't know what this means in the context of a relationship; so, based on my lived experience, I'd recommend turning the oven off, opening the window, and apologizing to the neighbors.

Quantum Dating: I am not Gen Z, I do not get it.

Tuning: What?

Shack Packing-ing: This sounds like a B-52s song.

Delaytionship: Who comes up with these terms?

Situationing: My head hurts.

Submarining: I'm so old.

Married: Oh, okay!! This one I know! Hire Laura Dern. Haven't you seen *Marriage Story*?

Congratulations! You just successfully exited your relationship, regardless of what kind of relationship it was! And just remember—relationships don't fail. They successfully terminate.

Things My Exes Have Ruined for Me

Every relationship ruins *something* for me, no matter how good it was while it lasted. There's just *one thing* I can no longer enjoy simply because it reminds me too much of an ex. Here are a few:

The Simpsons: My college partner and I used to watch *The Simpsons* every night, and now I can't enjoy it without thinking of them. In fact, nuclear power plants in general make me cry. (Well, they make my eyes well up—I hope it's tears.)

Michael Cera: I dated a guy once who looked exactly like Michael Cera (yes, from time to time I do date hot men), and now I can't even watch *Juno* without remembering Dave dumping me at my sister's graduation. Fortunately, Michael Cera's career never fully recovered from his choice to grow a mustache in 2012, so it doesn't come up that much anymore.

Fedoras: I'm humiliated to say that Jeff wore a fedora every day, and since the breakup, the little caps have completely stopped turning me on the way they used to.

The *Atlantic*: Did you have to send me eight articles to read? Would seven not have been enough?

Women Named "Karen": I swipe no on all of them now—they could all be her. And you can imagine how damaging the meme was to my mental health.

Bad Sex: Troy was so bad in bed, and I miss him with every fiber of my being. Two weeks ago, I slept with someone who went down on me as though my pussy were a corn dog, and I burst into tears. It was so awkward explaining to them that it wasn't their fault—it was just that they were so bad in bed, which made me miss Troy. They did nothing wrong, they just triggered me.

Fights: They were *our* special thing. Since Stacy left, I'll never enjoy throwing a plate again.

Unbearable Assholes: Cam, my most recent ex, was an unbearable asshole and they're dead to me now. This is especially a problem because some of my *best friends* are unbearable assholes.

Asparagus: It used to be my favorite food, but Freddy looked exactly like one. Sigh. I *really* need to stop dating hot men.

....

Was the Breakup Mutual?—A True-Crime Investigation

How can you ever really know if a breakup is mutual? Is it based on what the couple says happened, or what friends think the real story was? Does "mutual" mean that they both felt the exact same way about the relationship ending, or did one just agree to call it "mutual" for PR reasons? Are they still sleeping together? And is this any of my business?

Navid and Sam were a typical couple. They were in a relationship, and they did couple-y things like do sex and hold hands and smile in public collaboratively. You know—normal stuff. Everything seemed fine. Until one day, while I was minding my own business, Sam showed up as a potential Hinge match on my phone. How?!! What happened to Navid? I wanted to get to the bottom of it.

"What happened to Navid? I want to get to the bottom of it," I messaged Sam. Sam had been eager enough to talk to me that they'd matched me back, so I must be the right person to lead this investigation.

"We broke up. It was mutual," Sam responded.

Unsatisfied with that response, I began to hunt for more information. I couldn't quite wrap my head around how a breakup could *truly* be mutual. I'd always imagined mutual breakups were when two people said, "I think we should break up!" at the exact same moment and then both yelled, "JINX!!!" But that seemed unlikely, as Sam was generally soft-spoken, and I couldn't picture them yelling. More likely than not, one of them dumped the other. And I intended to get to the bottom of it. So I started this podcast.

For the last eighteen months, I've spent every working day trying to find out if the breakup of Navid T. and Sam R. was *actually* mutual. And if not—who dumped whom?

To get to the bottom of things, let's start at the beginning. Exactly when did this breakup happen?

On November 17, 2020, Sam sent a text to their friend Stevie that read, "Hey, Navid and I are done, can I come over for ice cream?" Stevie responded affirmatively. I've been unable to gain access to more of their texts, as Stevie slammed her laptop shut when she realized I was reading them over her shoulder in our company's budget meeting. I found this to be an overreaction, as Clarence was complaining that we spent too much on ink cartridges. There was no reason for Stevie to add drama to an already tense conversation.

Still, it seemed like Sam and Navid's story wasn't adding up. The relationship had ended, but no one would tell me who dumped whom. I needed to speak with an expert witness.

Missy K. tweets about dating and has a following of over 1,800, so I figured she'd be a good person to ask.

"Missy, what's the benefit of saying a breakup was mutual?" I asked her. "I know so many people do this, and I'm not sure I fully understand why."

"It's simple," said Missy. She had an airy confidence that only comes from having so many Twitter followers. "You say it's mutual if you either got dumped, or dumped someone in a mean way that you don't want to own up to. Like, if you dump them on the day of their grandma's funeral, then yeah, say it's mutual."

My interaction with Missy left me with more questions than answers. Did either Sam or Navid dump the other in a particularly cruel way? Or were they embarrassed to be dumped? How was I going to find out? Also, would Missy be willing to retweet this podcast episode when it was out? I only had fourteen followers.

Speaking of which, Sam never responded to my next Hinge message, asking if they wanted to get a drink. Mysteries upon mysteries upon mysteries.

In my experience, it seemed like whoever was less into the relationship was more likely to have initiated the breakup. Or were they? My experience, admittedly, is not very reliable, as I'm fortunate enough to never have been in the situation in which I had to deal with initiating a breakup. I must dig further.

I'd like to take a break to thank the podcast's official sponsors—my parents—for making this lifestyle possible. The couch in your basement is definitely not bad, and I appreciate having a place to stay. Also, the eclair in the freezer is mine. This ad is to confirm that you're listening to this podcast—if the eclair is gone, you don't love me enough. Love, Max.

Next, I threw myself into my research to determine who was more into Sam and Navid's relationship. I asked every single one of their friends if they knew who liked the other more. All of them said that was a rude question. People have no appreciation for my genre.

"The breakup was mutual, they really respect each other," said Tina, the rare friend willing to serve the public by helping me get to the bottom of things. "The time had just come."

But *what* time had come? She didn't say. Time was always coming and going, that's how I ended up being thirty-three. I needed more specifics.

I figured some of my past relationships could offer some clues. I had to get to the bottom of it.

I reached out to my ex to see if she wanted to get back together, but she declined to comment. I was at a complete loss—my investigation was going nowhere.

"WHOSE FAULT WAS IT?!!?!?!" I bellowed into the void, *Garden State*–style. All I heard back was, *Whose fault was it?*, which was my original question. Get your own question, void.

I thought about what I knew about Navid and Sam. They'd been dating. They were in a relationship. Then they stopped being in a relationship. They were no longer in each other's Instagram stories. Navid followed at least one twenty-one-year-old woman on Instagram, but she had the same last name as him. A cousin, or did he already find someone new and marry? I saw Sam on Hinge. They said the breakup was mutual. They seemed to respect each other, from the fact that neither had posted nudes of the other to Reddit (and I read *all* of Reddit). None of these facts added up. The bottom of it—I was going to get there.

"What's your alibi?" I texted Navid one night.

"I don't need an alibi. Our breakup is actually none of your business," Navid texted back.

"Okay, but what were you doing at the time you had a mutual breakup? I have to get to the bottom of it."

Navid didn't text back. The message didn't show that it had been delivered. Weird—I contacted Apple Support. I had to get to the bottom of it.

"This happens if your number has been blocked," a customer service agent wrote back.

How'd my number get blocked? The questions kept piling on. Would I ever get to the bottom of it?

And then, the unthinkable happened.

I received a text from Stevie at 6:58 p.m. "Hey, stop texting Sam and Navid. They just decided to get back together, and honestly, your whole investigation has been kinda weird. You were never even friends with either of them, you just met them once at my housewarming and started following them on Instagram."

She was right. I did get invited to a housewarming party, one time, once, and I'd love to be invited again.

"Was the getting back together mutually agreed upon?" I asked Stevie.

She never responded.

On Season 2, tune in as I finally get to the bottom of things. Well, rock bottom, according to my therapist. Until next time, Dump-erinos—stay single.

A Love Worth Writing a *New York Times* Modern Love Piece About: A Submission to the *New York Times* Modern Love Column

A woman commits herself to getting published in Modern Love, and her romantic life takes a toll. Upon further reflection, she realizes it probably would have taken a toll anyway.

What does it *mean* to be published in Modern Love? Was your love life so fascinating that your story had to be shared? Had you long since set aside your life dreams of novel-writing, only to return to it when your loved one got diagnosed with a rare genetic disorder? Or were you just better than me?

In my quest for the truth, I returned time and time again to one core question—could publication in Modern Love be brute-forced, if I simply tried hard enough to make my love life profound? Could I craft my love life in such a way that I would—someday—earn a spot in this revered column? And if so, how?

In retrospect, making it into Modern Love was a fire that burned within me from a young age, much like a yeast infection. I met Javier when I was seventeen. It was a love forbidden by our families—a classic Romeo and Juliet situation, just like the Taylor Swift song. He lived in Scarsdale, and I in White Plains. We had no way of seeing each other (our families didn't take issue with it, but we'd both failed our road tests earlier that summer). We met only twice, both times on the Metro-North, and as I looked into his deep, brown eyes—no, wait, *hazel*—I thought, I could write 1,700 words about you.

I left for college with Javier on my mind. Was it real love? Would he still try to sleep with me at Thanksgiving? He never had before, but there's a first time for everything! Or was there someone better for me out there, like a partner who I didn't have to pass my road test for? More specifically, despite our incompatibilities, could I craft a compelling narrative about him, such that I could find my way into the Style section's sumptuous pages?

"'Sumptuous' doesn't really make sense in that context," my new dorm mates told me, but I didn't heed their warnings. Three months later, I was rejected for the very first time and had already forgotten Javier's last name. It's been a roller coaster ever since.

I've submitted to Modern Love thirty-six times. Every three months for the past twelve years. The editor might not know me by name, but he, surely, knows me by profligate comma use, I think, right? I've committed my whole heart to getting accepted by Modern Love, which is why I now feel comfortable writing a Modern Love submission about trying to get published in Modern Love. It has been, in many ways, the greatest romantic pursuit of my life.

I know what you're thinking—you've dated thirty-six people? No, it's not that simple. Some of them offered multiple stories for me to milk. Fred, for example, was the first man I met off Tinder—an exciting foray into online dating that spawned the pitch "A Man Worth Clicking On, and Then Clicking For" (Fred didn't know how to use his garage door opener). Later, Fred would become the first and only man I ever pegged, which gave birth to, "A Man Worth Being Penetrated By, and Then Penetrating." Fred also suggested we move in together, but I had to decline, as I had already written a moving-in piece about Darla: "My Partner Said We Shouldn't Live Together. I Felt Differently," in which I thought Darla and I should live together, but she felt differently. Darla was also the subject of one of my all-time favorite pieces, "Knitting, Fermenting, Chugging Cold Brew to Feel Like I'm in Love, and Vacuuming—the Hobbies I Develop in the Wake of My Breakup." The piece was rejected, but I lost seven pounds (food poisoning from the fermented cabbage).

I've proven myself willing to jump off bridges to find a love story interesting enough for a Modern Love column. Indeed, please see the piece I submitted in February 2014, "He Was a Bungee Jumper. I Liked to Have Both Feet on the Ground." I'm always on the hunt for a good story. If ever I find myself swiping through Hinge and I see a person whose profile is a complete enigma, I ask them out immediately. I can't recommend this practice at all. In fact, I would urge you to categorically swipe left on anyone who lists their profession as "entrepreneur," without clarifying what they're the entrepreneur of. I expanded on this theory in, "When His Mom's Basement Is His Start-up Incubator."

Devoting myself to Modern Love hasn't come without a price. For one thing, an intern at the *New York Times* informed me that I'm going to have to start paying $10 per submission if I want to continue, as it's become burdensome for the editor. Furthermore, I sometimes have to make sacrifices to get the story I want.

In, "Is He the One, or Is He Just the First Guy I've Slept with in Three Years Who Cleans His Toilet?" I discuss my budding romance with the plumber Mark DeDario.

Mark was kind, sweet, and seemingly unburdened by the fact that I was still spending every afternoon standing outside my ex-ex-lover's house, in order to put the final touches on a piece entitled, "Standing Outside Her House for Four Months Didn't Make Her Love Me. Neither Did Adopting a Ferret." Mark *wanted* the relationship to move forward. Unlike all my exes, who did not, as covered in my piece, "After Fourteen Ex-Partners Tell You the Problem Is You, Could It Be Time to Look Inward?" I thought Mark was the one, but I also didn't think I'd know for *sure* until I'd sent the relationship up in flames, for narrative reasons. In writing it, I concluded that he *was* the one. Unfortunately, he'd since stopped returning my calls.

But as much as I've given up in my pursuit of Modern Love, I've also reaped great rewards. I now know eighty-five synonyms for "tragic," and I can write coherent prose in the midst of devastating (which you may notice is a common synonym for "tragic") breakups. And there's a certain harmony to the whole experience—almost all of my thirty-six essays have dealt with my romantic rejection, and all thirty-six of them have been rejected by the editor of Modern Love. As a romance writer, I now notice that type of symmetry. I've grown really observant.

Before I finish, I should pose a few more questions to the reader. Who? What? Where? When? *Why?*

This piece isn't going to last 1,700 words. I could choose to add some filler—perhaps regale you with tales of other publications I've been rejected from, including but not limited to *Cosmo,* the *Washington Post,* and *Golfer's Digest* (my ex, Rudolf, loved to swing. I would later learn that he didn't mean golf, but that didn't stop me from investing in $1,400 clubs). But I won't, because in writing all these rejected Modern Love pitches, I've perhaps learned the greatest lesson of all: My exes were right: I should write less. They were referring to the way I text—which I cover in "He Said Stop Texting, But I Texted Anyway"—but still. It all comes full circle, in the end.

And so . . . you're probably wondering what happened to Javier after that summer. I don't know, but I know this much—his name was actually Todd. Because I *know* how to tell a story.

The Friend Zone

INT. COFFEE SHOP—DAY

(STACY and MARK sit and sip lattes.)

STACY: What are you still doing here?

MARK: Dating you!

STACY: I said we should just be friends.

MARK: Oh, I thought you were just quoting *The Social Network*.

STACY: I would never. But I actually just sold this company, and you know what's cooler than a million do—

MARK: I have to go. I can't believe you'd do this to me. On my *birthday*.

INT. FRANK'S APARTMENT—NIGHT

(FRANK and a bunch of MARK's other friends are hiding behind couches and inside vents and stuff like that. A big sign hangs over the door that says, "Welcome to the Friend Zone!" FRANK turns to DAMON.)

FRANK: Do you think the sign is clear?

DAMON: Yes, of course. It's a *zone* full of *friends*. For his birthday party. What's not to get?

FRANK: I don't know . . . I feel like "Friend Zone" sometimes means something else? But I can't remember.

DAMON: It's a *zone* full of *friends*. It's clearly a good thing. It's like Chuck E. Cheese.

FRANK: Mark is lactose intolerant.

DAMON: I said *like* Chuck E. Cheese.

(MARK opens the door. Everyone jumps out from their hiding place.)

FRANK AND FRIENDS: SURPRISE!!!

(MARK bursts into tears.)

FRANK: What happened?!!

MARK: I just got dumped, and then you go and make this sign. . . .

(MARK gestures to the "Friend Zone" sign and continues to sob.)

FRANK: Shit. Oh, fuck. I remember what "Friend Zone" means.

DAMON: Damn, yeah, I forgot that the opposite of getting laid is being a friend.

FRANK: Okay, everybody, let's take the sign down.

(All of MARK's friends hang their heads in shame and tear down the decorations before leaving the party, one by one.)

In Which Barbie Tells Ken She's Looking for a Man with Bendier Arms

Dear Ken, I'm sorry to say I don't think things between us are working out. I hate to be the bearer of bad news, but I've changed as a person, and this relationship is no longer the right fit for me. Because of how serious we've gotten, mostly due to the imagination of young girls, I feel that I owe you an explanation. The time has come for me to find a doll with slightly bendier arms. It's just, like, I want to learn how to cook, you know?

I love you, but I'm not *in love* with you. I guess being *in love* might come easier to dolls with flat feet (they're more grounded, by definition). I think we might be better as friends, and if not that, at least as peaceful cohabitants in Laney's toy chest. I mean, we know each other so well—I've looked at you from exactly two different angles, based on the degree to which my head can tilt—and we've been together since the sixties. I can't imagine life without you, or life at all, since I'm inanimate. Still, at the end of the day, you wouldn't be able to tie my shoelaces if you tried, and that's sort of a deal-breaker for me.

It's not you, it's me. I'm sorry for using such a cliché breakup line, it's just the one that was programmed into me. But you know I love change—I was an astronaut and a firefighter and the first female president of the United States of America, all without breaking a sweat. But you weren't even able to take a polaroid of the inauguration because of your arms. So, I guess, it's actually you.

I treasure the memories we shared—that sweet dream house, discoing, being blond, our matching monogrammed swimsuits (I mean, how many guys would be open to something as cheesy as that?), going to prom, being even blonder, and then going to prom again in our late 50s as part of a rebrand. It's all been such a blast. I literally did not stop smiling the whole time. I just really need to work on myself right now. Like, I've started doing yoga to see if I can one day get my heels to touch the ground. I can't make myself more flexible when you won't bend at all for me—I'm sorry.

I guess at the end of the day, I just really hope you don't take this personally. It's not your fault your arms don't bend at all—that's just the way Mattel made you. And even if it weren't, you'd still be the product of social conditioning that teaches men not to cry or bend their arms, so I wouldn't hold it against you. And I can't imagine it's that bad for you either. I mean, we didn't have much of a sex life. As they always say— having sex is like riding a bicycle: They haven't yet made a Barbie that can do it.

We're just looking for different things right now. Like, we're on two completely different paths. Specifically, Devon put me on his porch, and Cara left you in the trunk of her parents' car. You'll never be able to climb out and find me, because besides your arms' inability to bend, you also don't even have opposable thumbs.

I need a doll who's more my speed. I'm looking for the real deal, someone with bendy arms who knows how to use them. Bendy arms seem really great for so many reasons, and I intend to find out all of them. That's why I'm dating Woody now. He's floppy everywhere. So you see, I've moved on.

I'm sorry we had to let a lack of bendy arms get in the way of a good thing, but in my defense, your arms are also *really* short. It's weird, Ken. It's always been weird.

Yelp Reviews of Breakups

⭐⭐⭐⭐⭐

5 stars: I'd heard good things from friends about being dumped by Sarah, and I understand why. She clearly stated her intention—to terminate our relationship. When I asked follow-up questions (Did she really mean it, Would she reconsider in several weeks, Did it have anything to do with the TikTok fight I got in with her 13-year-old cousin), she answered each one with poise and grace. She also confirmed she didn't know about the TikTok fight.

⭐⭐⭐⭐☆

4 stars: I liked the ambience of this breakup. Parker made his bed before inviting me over to dump me, which is the type of thoughtfulness he showed throughout the relationship. Like the time I got the flu, he texted, "bummer, hope you feel ok :/". He also gave me a Kind bar before I left. Well, I took it from his kitchen, but still. I'd happily get dumped by him again, assuming he's stocked up. I subtract one point because he did still dump me, which was not what I wanted, but no one's perfect.

⭐⭐⭐☆☆

3 stars: Liza's breakup was a bit out of the way. She drove me to Big Sur to announce she couldn't see us ever living together, not now, not in a year, not ever. I appreciated the calming, majestic views—mostly of her face, since she very sweetly put a genuine effort into seeming sad—as she crushed my entire soul. Unfortunately, I have to subtract three points because we then had to drive all the way back to San Francisco in silence. I add one point back on because she let me pick the music.

2 stars: I hated the service. Specifically, the phone service. How am I supposed to handle being dumped if I can't immediately post a picture of me crying on my Instagram story for my last four sexual partners to see? Other than that, the breakup was *okay*, only because Sam refrained from using the phrase "It's not you, it's me." I do wonder if it was me. I mean, he eventually did clarify that it was, but still—some things we just aren't meant to know, as I said. "It was definitely you," he responded.

1 star: Juan's breakup is really not what it used to be. I've been dumped by him many times, and the old leadership was clearly much more effective—I left unsure about whether or not we were still in a relationship. He kept using aphorisms I didn't understand, like "The grass is always greener on the other side," and "Two's company, three's a crowd." He never clarified who the "third" was. When I asked if things were "over over," he said, "Never say never," followed by, "but yes." I texted him later to say he used to be much better at dumping me, and I just wanted things to go back to the way they used to be. He hasn't responded. I'd get back together with him, but I will *never* break up with him again.

0 stars: I'm not the type to leave nasty Yelp reviews, but I feel that I need to share. I'd give 0 stars for ghosting and ghosting alone. Grow up, Steve!

0 stars: Also, text messages to end a three-year-long relationship. Grow up, Kate!

0 stars: And also for times I thought we were going to be together forever. Grow up, Ty! If you're trying to run a successful and well-reviewed business, be an adult and marry me!

Checklist for Your Breakup

So your relationship is over? Here is a helpful checklist for those who may be feeling lost in their newfound singlehood:

- ☐ Take two weeks off social media, except to occasionally post a sad song lyric from a '90s band, so people know *something* is up, but not what specifically. Be careful, though—one of your Reply Guys will inevitably comment with the dictionary.com definition of "lonely" if you do the Backstreet Boys ballad.

- ☐ Send a string of sad emojis to your best friend. Wait for her to guess that you're sad because of the breakup, and then accuse her of never having supported the relationship to begin with.

- ☐ Decide whether you should say it's mutual. Just know that if you do this, you will both look like you got dumped.

- ☐ Personally text all your exes. Not everyone does this step, but I've found it really helpful and cleansing. If they never knew you'd been in a relationship, don't bring it up—it's hotter if you're being random.

- ☐ It's time to put feelers out for someone new. Start liking all of Henry Golding's Instagram photos.

- ☐ Tell your boss you won't be coming in to work the next day. You do this every Wednesday, but now you have an excuse.

☐ Download Hinge, if you don't have it. I usually skip this step, as I'm rarely optimistic enough to delete it in the first place.

☐ Assign blame to whoever had the idea to date in the first place. None of this would have happened if they hadn't sent you that text after you vomited up cheese fries at Daryl's party last year.

☐ Decide who won. This is the most important step, particularly for crafting a narrative going forward, and you absolutely *must* agree on it.

☐ Describe your bowel movements to them in great detail. This is your one last chance to dig into your all-time favorite conversation topic with the one person who ever pretended to care, and the stakes have never been lower.

Who I Consider My "Ex"

Okay, wow. I just learned that "ex" is short for "ex-partner" or "ex-boyfriend" or "ex-girlfriend." I find that extremely limiting—there's no reason someone should have to have been my official partner for me to dramatically refer to them as my "ex." In my opinion, "ex" is an umbrella term, including but not limited to:

- The person I was in a relationship with for three years

- The person I was in a relationship with for two years

- The person I was *definitely* in a relationship with, even though they refused to put labels on it

- The person my mom would always refer to as my partner, and I'd always have to say, "Mom, you know Steve and I are just friends who do unreciprocated oral on the weekends." Silly Mom.

- The person I slept with on-and-off for a year

- The person I slept with consistently for a few months

- The person I slept with on-and-off for a weekend (one total instance)

- The person I would have slept with, if they'd asked

- The person I went on three dates with last year

- The person I went on two dates with over the course of four years

- My broken Roomba

- The person who I was going to go on a date with, but I had a family emergency at the last minute (my sister informed me she was canceling her Disney+, and I had to watch *Hamilton* that night or never). We could have rescheduled, but I didn't want to.

- The person I matched with on Hinge who never messaged me

- Anyone who's ever liked one tweet and then not liked the next one. This behavior is simply cruel.

- Some of my old cell phones. Others, I never felt bonded to in the first place.

- The person I made eye contact with after a meditation session. If I'm in a spiritual place, it's a relationship. And once you break eye contact—it's over.

- The person I made eye contact with at the grocery store one time. If I'm in a place full of food, it's a relationship.

- The person I don't really know but wanted to give more character to in the story I'm telling. "Ex" seems better than "acquaintance"— I want the listener to know I am a woman scorned.

- Half the people in memes we don't see anymore

- Several TV characters. When Steve Carell randomly left *The Office*— that was a breakup.

- Jeff. I won't explain.

- The person reading this

- Manny, who hates that I call him an ex, as he is my partner at present. I've always been forward-thinking.

Drafts of Eulogies I've Written for My Past Partners to Give at My Funeral (Including Their Edits, Which I Did Not Approve but Have No Power to Cut, as I Would Be Dead at Time of Delivery, at Which Point I Would Unfortunately Be Unable to Continue Giving Them Instructions)

Thank you all for gathering here today to remember the life of Ginny. I dated Ginny from 2018 to 2020, and I consider those the best years of my life. Physically—I did an Iron Man. I know the ending came as a shock, since Ginny was so young, but I had to move on to someone I could see myself settling down with, who had a more regular view of clipping toenails— Oh, you meant her death. Yes, she was almost too young for that, too. My life will be forever changed.

Today, may we honor the spirit of Ginny. In the eight months that I dated Ginny, she regularly woke me up at 5 a.m. to remind me of her unusual circadian rhythm. For a woman who woke up before dawn, she accomplished very little. She lived life to the fullest by being awake so often, doing God knows what. I will miss her forever—keep them awake in Heaven, you sleep-deprived—sorry, am I reading this correctly?—goddess.

As many of you know, Ginny and I dated from sophomore year of college to later in sophomore year of college. Ginny was one of my earliest girlfriends, but not my least memorable. No, that title goes to Millie, who's actually here with us today. Hello, Millie. You're looking well.

Ginny once made a joke about me doing an autopsy on her pussy, so I think she was ready to go. She was loved and respected by all she casually slept with, myself included. May you rest in peace, you beautiful wit. See—I kept part of what you wrote, in case you're listening.

Ginny and I met on Hinge last year and casually dated for a month before deciding we were better as friends. We haven't hung out since, and I'm simply beside myself with the news that she's gone. The angels will now be looking after her, which is good, because Ginny generally doesn't cope well with being alone, which she told me nineteen times, as I tried to break up with her.

Ginny was the best I ever had. Sorry, let me rewrite what she gave me. Ginny was the best I ever had, she said.

A butterfly flapping its wings in Texas may cause a hurricane in a Lemony Snicket novel, which is to say, Ginny changed me, in the way everyone does. The wedding weekend I spent with her was not bad, for a wedding.

Ginny and I had sex on my roommate's futon last weekend because my cousin was sleeping in my bed. We'd met three hours earlier. I just have no idea how I'm going to get by without her. Ginny was really, truly perfect and she really, truly wrote this eulogy. She said she'd never had a sexual partner she'd fought so little with, even though we'd only known each other six hours, and we did fight. Which is to say—she was a fighter, right until the very end.

Ginny's casket is then marched down the aisle, carried by all her ex-lovers, to a slow rendition of "Blank Space" by Taylor Swift.

I have friends who've been engaged for years, which is wild to me because I could never commit to anyone for that long. And I have friends who've gotten married, which is crazy to me because did no one tell them there are other options, like breaking up? And I have friends who've gotten married after asserting for years that they "didn't believe in marriage" which is just nutso to me, because why did I spend $200 on a fictional blender for your fictional wedding, if it's all just fantasy? And my friend Clara is even looking into *preschools*, which is so mind-blowingly *bananas* to me, because I did that when I was three. I guess she's moving slower than me, and that's okay. We're all at different life stages.

On the one hand, it's normal to me that relationships progress and people move in together, get married, have kids, learn how to properly clean a dishwasher, etc. On the other, it's all so strange when considered in the context of modern dating. Do you mean to tell me the guy I'm currently splitting $2 tacos with while he tells me about his favorite memes (that meme that's a "baked potato," like a potato smoking weed—have you seen it??) might one day be responsible for me *adding a new person to the world*? Sorry, but that's a little far-fetched.

You may start to feel distant from your friends who are at different phases of their dating journeys because they've made different choices. But that's all they are— choices. We can make whichever ones suit our needs best, and there are a million and a half ways for your life to progress without committing to a long-term relationship and/or starting a family and/or acquiring a menagerie of small pets and plants. That being said, if "getting serious" is for you, go for it. Serious relationships may lead to dog-ownership, and I'm down to dog-sit for you.

An Unfortunately Realistic Move-in Talk

INT. ERIK'S BEDROOM—DAY

(The bedroom is dimly lit, and a towel seems to be the current stand-in for a rug. The bed appears to be full-sized, but it could conceivably be a twin, or possibly one of those in-between type beds they make for children or grown men who act as such. Clothes are strewn all over the floor. It's unclear whether the items are clean or dirty, but what is clear: ERIK picks his outfits off of the rug. He's rummaging through shirts, while TANYA sits on the bed.)

TANYA: Hey, babe, we should talk.

ERIK: About what happened at the strip club? I said sorry—how was I supposed to know that's what a lap dance was.

TANYA: No, no, about that other thing. My lease is up at the end of the month.

(ERIK looks up, confused, like a deer in headlights.)

ERIK: Wait, but don't you need a lease for . . . living there?

TANYA: Yeah, but I was thinking I could . . . you know . . . I don't even have a kitchen.

ERIK: Do you really want to move back in with your parents?

TANYA: That's not what I meant . . .

(ERIK returns to rummaging through his clothing. He seems to be looking for a sock to match the white one he's holding.)

TANYA: Okay, you know how I pay $3,300 a month to live in a shoebox, and you pay $459,033 a month to live in an even smaller shoebox?

ERIK: I love NYC.

TANYA: Same. But there's a way we could get a slightly larger shoebox, and each only pay, like $3,000 a month. Wouldn't that be better?

(ERIK looks up. He pauses for a long time.)

ERIK: I mean, I don't even have a shower.

TANYA: You actually do.

(A beat.)

ERIK: Can you show me where?

TANYA: Yes, but let's have this conversation first.

ERIK: Let me just find a sock.

(ERIK keeps rummaging around.)

TANYA: You won't find it until you put your clothes away! Which you barely have space to do here! We need to talk about this!

(ERIK holds up a red sock triumphantly, even though it doesn't match the other one he's wearing.)

ERIK: Sure I do!

TANYA: That's a beanie.

(ERIK examines it. It is a beanie. He puts it on his head. TANYA looks at him intensely. It's unclear if she's mad or just thinks he's dumb, or both. She then stands and takes his hands.)

TANYA: Erik, I feel ready. To take the next step. To have an apartment with a window. To only have two insect infestations a year—seven, max. To have a fridge that works, sometimes, so the only reason we have to throw out all our kale is because we haven't eaten it. Erik, I like you so much, and my apartment has mold in it. I think we've been dating long enough that it could be time to ask the question—should we move in together, for logistical reasons only?

(ERIK is stoic. He turns back to the clothes on his floor.)

ERIK: I thought that might be where this conversation was headed.

TANYA: You mean because I texted you, "Can we talk about moving in together for logistical reasons only?"

ERIK: But we've only been together seven years.

TANYA (*to herself*): My mom says men get better in their late seventies. I can stick it out.

ERIK: If we do this, will I have to pick my clothes up off the floor?

TANYA: Remember what I said when you asked me that same question, before we decided you could have a drawer at my apartment?

ERIK and TANYA (*in unison*): Yes.

TANYA: And look what happened—it turned out fine.

(They both look down at the floor, covered in clothing.)

ERIK: Okay! I'm in!

(TANYA gets off the bed to embrace him, but she slips on a sock. They laugh, and laugh, and laugh.)

Don't Get Married before You've Lived Together

Don't get married before you live together. You just never know what the other person will be like to live with, and you need to figure that out before marriage.

Definitely don't tie the knot until you've traveled together. You absolutely *must* find out if your future spouse is a good travel companion—what if you get married and then learn that they cry during turbulence but not during *The Notebook*? If you don't have money to travel, simply hitchhike together and see how your partner reacts when they have a gun to their head. This is good for knowing what they'll be like with your parents.

You need to make sure your marriage can withstand major life changes, so don't get married until one of you has been fired from their job. If you like your job, then plan to marry someone who's bad at theirs. Marriage is about compromise.

Don't get married before you've had children together. Seeing what the other person is like as a parent is key to determining whether they're the right person for you. If it turns out they're a completely negligent parent, at least you know before you do something extreme like buying a dress. Your mom can always raise the tester baby— that's why you call her *Mom*.

And don't get married before you've both gone through periods of extreme depression. If your other half isn't a naturally depressed person, try to induce it by depriving them of food and sleep. You need to know what they're like when they're *really* down before your parents let you use their yard for a wedding.

What if weddings just aren't for you? You need to find that out before you marry your partner, so don't get married until you've married someone else first. Please consider me for the role of your starter bride. And then don't get divorced—it's a turnoff to future lovers, and a bureaucratic nightmare.

And definitely, definitely, definitely don't get married before you've watched the other person die. Honestly, that's a really traumatic event in a marriage, and you want to make sure you can handle it before you commit to spending your whole life together. Don't be selfish—bravely volunteer yourself as the one to watch your partner meet their maker. This is usually the step where couples realize it's not going to work out, so make sure not to skip it.

(originally seen on mcsweeneys.net)

Makes Me Laugh

Once upon a time, there was a pretty, pretty princess named Damsel. No, she wasn't from a royal family and no, she didn't have any magical powers. But she celebrated her birthday for an entire month, so "princess" was the only appropriate way to describe her.

That wasn't the only princesslike thing about her, though. You see, Damsel had been Cursed. Damsel lived in the beautiful kingdom of Los Angeles, and Damsel wanted to find her Prince Charming. Or at least—*a* Prince Charming. Or anybody charming—they were surprisingly hard to find, even in the city of aspiring TV stars. Damsel hadn't had much luck finding him, even though she told her Court of Admirers (a term her sorority sisters disputed) that she wasn't terribly picky. Because Damsel's Curse was that she only wanted one thing. And until she got that thing, she would never be able to get serious with anybody.

"All I want is a partner who makes me laugh," Damsel said again and again and again. "Just someone who makes me laugh. And then I will have found the One. And then I will settle down, forever. I want to find the One, and they must be funny."

Damsel had never been able to find someone she could settle down with. She wanted to badly, but she wasn't willing to sway from her one criterion. And thanks to the Curse, she wasn't even able.

"So you want, like, the court jester?" her Court of Admirers asked.

"Yes, that would be perfect," Damsel responded.

"It's too bad this isn't an actual kingdom, or we could totally get you a court jester. You may have to settle for a stand-up comedian," they said.

"No, someone who makes me laugh," Damsel responded.

"What about Troy?" they asked. "He made you laugh."

"No, he was a tickler," said Damsel. She found tickling to be the oddest experience of all—you could smile so much while being deeply uncomfortable. Much like watching stand-up comedy.

"What about Nancy?" they asked. "She made you laugh."

"No, I've outgrown thinking farts are funny." Nancy had poor digestion.

"What about Peyton?" they asked. "He made you laugh."

"No, I can't just be taking nitrous oxide all the time." Peyton was a dentist.

Damsel's Court of Admirers felt sorry for her. They were familiar with her Curse.

How had Damsel been afflicted with this Curse? One day, many years ago, she was watching cartoons and one of the characters slipped on a banana peel. She erupted into a fit of laughter and then thought, Wow—this is the best feeling in the world. I must chase this and only this until the end of time. (Damsel had not yet tried drugs.) And that's the day the Curse came to be. Find the one who makes ye laugh, and only then will thee settle down.

The princess's Curse had taken her on many a misfortunate adventure. It wasn't that she was unable to find anyone who made her laugh—it's that in only caring about that, she often found people who weren't otherwise suited for serious relationships.

Take Mark, whom she'd picked up at an improv show. He was forty years old and still did improv, so that wasn't great. There was Tracy, who was so obsessed with verbally editing her witty tweets that she had a hard time listening. She didn't have any interest in a relationship—she was more concerned with internet fame. Lastly, there was Seth Rogen. While he did make her laugh, she ultimately couldn't handle the limelight. Dating Seth Rogen is harder than Charlize Theron makes it seem.

But despite all this hardship, Damsel kept going, dating miserable funny person after miserable funny person. She was unhappy, her abs hurt but in an unfulfilling way, she never felt comfortable around her partners, and she hadn't had a serious conversation about the future in years. She did their laundry and made them dinner and wondered whether one of these funny, funny people would ever want to get serious and produce an heir to the throne. Someone had to take over her fiefdom (Damsel was likely to inherit her uncle's Subaru).

"No," said Byron, her most recent lover, when she brought up the topic of reproduction. "Kids are funnier than me. I can't handle the competition."

He was right. Kids were funnier than him.

But Damsel had steeled herself. Like many young royals trying to navigate the dating pool, she was Cursed with looking for exactly one criterion in a partner, and myopically moving toward that one goal without ever giving the slightest consideration to her underlying happiness. Damsel was miserable, but at least she was focused.

"What about someone kind?" her Court of Admirers asked.

"No, then I'll feel guilty when I'm mean to them," she said.

"What about someone easy to be around?" they said.

"I like a challenge," she responded. "That's why I'm on a beanstalk-only cleanse right now."

"What about someone with a job?" they said.

"I want someone who can spend all their time with me," she replied.

"There are other good feelings besides laughter," they said. "What about someone who makes you drunk?"

"I'll keep that in mind for later," said Damsel. "If the laughing thing doesn't work out. But for now—I must stay the course."

Damsel wrote out a to-do list. *Find the One. Laugh. Settle Down. Keep Laughing.*

Oh! Poor Damsel! She'd met so many funny people, but she wasn't finding anyone ideal for a relationship—so sad! All she had to do to break the Curse was to open her mind and drop her one criterion. Sadly, she didn't know that! If only she had a Fairy Godmother to steer her! If only, if only!

One afternoon, Damsel was walking in the Enchanted Park when she came across a woman crying on a bench.

Women deserve to cry in public without being interrupted, Damsel thought. I'll say nothing.

"Why are you ignoring me?" the crying woman asked.

"Oh, sorry," said Damsel awkwardly. "What's . . . uh . . . what's up?"

"I'm fighting with my boyfriend. I always thought he was so perfect, because I thought I was just looking for someone who made a lot of money, but he turned out to be a bit of a dick."

"Oh," said Damsel. "That sucks." She sympathized with the woman's plight, to an extent, but also, she loved money. I mean, she was a princess.

"I guess that's the problem with always dating the same type of person, and always looking for the exact same thing, instead of adjusting my preferences when it doesn't work out."

"Yeah," said Damsel. "That is."

"I like your tiara," the woman sniffed. "Did you get it at Urban Outfitters?"

Damsel had gotten it at Urban Outfitters. The woman was very wise.

Damsel kept walking. She came across *another* woman crying in the Enchanted Park. Have we all synced up cycles? she wondered.

"What's wrong?" Damsel asked the crying woman, having learned her lesson last time.

"My partner dumped me. She said I fetishized her," the crying woman said.

"Did you?" Damsel asked.

"No! I just told her again and again and again that all I wanted was a partner who knew how to play Among Us. I thought I was making it clear I liked gamer girls!"

"Well, maybe she thought that was the only thing you liked about her," Damsel said.

"It was!" the woman responded.

Damsel didn't know what to say. She didn't know how to play Among Us, or any other video game for that matter. Damsel was relatively cool, despite having dated an improviser. So Damsel kept walking.

Finally, Damsel came across a couple in the Enchanted Park. Damsel was typically very envious of couples, as she, too, wanted a serious relationship. But not this couple. This couple was engaging in a duel. Okay, they were just yelling at each other, but still.

"I thought you were cool!" the man shouted at the woman.

"I am cool!" the woman responded.

"I told everyone you were cool! All I wanted was a partner who was cool! I just wanted someone cool, it was all I was looking for!" he said.

Wow, what an ogre, thought Damsel.

"You tried to fit me into a box! It's not my fault you were only ever looking for one thing in a partner. Why didn't you try to appreciate me for all of me? I'm smart, and kind, and I can cook, Darren! Why do you only insist on me being cool!?" the woman screamed.

"BECAUSE THAT'S WHAT I SAID I WANTED!!" shouted the man. "And you betrayed me!"

"HOW DID I BETRAY YOU?!" she screamed.

"You said you were cool! I was promised cool!"

"Grow up!! It was *one* Dave Matthews concert *one* time," the woman responded.

Damsel had to scurry away. She was completely shaken. The idea that someone you believed to be cool could turn around and go to a Dave Matthews concert . . . Thank goodness *she* didn't care about dating someone cool. She only cared about dating someone who made her laugh. Because that was her Curse.

Along with being Cursed, Damsel also had poor judgment, and she was bad at connecting ham-fisted prophetic declarations on benches to her own life. Even when they happened three times in a row, which is the perfect number of times for a parable. She didn't see herself in those people in the Enchanted Park, which was terribly bad luck.

Indeed, Damsel had a Fairy Godmother, and her Fairy Godmother *did* want to help her break the spell. She'd sent those people to her to teach her a lesson, but maybe she should have been there to walk Damsel through it. Unfortunately, Fairy Godmother wanted to work from home that day. We all deserve a chance to work from home every once in a while; I'm sure you'll agree.

So, the Curse persisted. Damsel continued to never, ever, ever, ever change what she was looking for in a partner. Not in the face of misery, new information, much better options, aggressive urging from her friends and family, and physical discomfort. Not in the face of sleeping with seventeen comedians who informed her that they couldn't settle down until they'd scored Netflix specials. No, she wanted someone who would make her laugh. Then—and only then—could she get serious. And as the days ticked by, Damsel's desire to get serious only grew and grew.

Where is he, she asked herself. Where is my Prince Charming, my laughter-inducing hero?

And then, she saw Daniel. Daniel wasn't good-looking, but he also wasn't smart. She saw him walking out of a bank. A bank with glass doors. That's right—Daniel walked right through the glass doors. Damsel burst out laughing. A real, genuine, non-laughing-gas, non-tickling laugh. She introduced herself to Daniel. And just like that, Damsel had found someone who really, truly made her laugh. Through all the tears of laughter, Damsel could see that Daniel was the one she could get serious with. She couldn't wait to tell her Court of Admirers she'd finally met the One (to be fair, she said this after every first date so they'd be sure to have a cute story for her wedding toast, but still).

As Daniel recovered from his accident (it was actually pretty bad—Damsel would later feel guilty for laughing so hard), she sat beside his bed. He was unconscious for the first two weeks. Two blissful weeks in which Damsel could gaze upon her partner and imagine their life together. In which she could dream about the future she'd always wanted. In which she could laugh.

One day, Daniel woke up. Under normal circumstances, this would have been a desirable outcome, but here was the problem: Daniel wasn't actually funny at all. No, he used the expression "thanks a latte" earnestly. His favorite form of comedy was Instagram meme pages. When he tried to tell jokes—which everyone discouraged—he told the punch line before the setup. He was objectively Not Funny. In fact, he was actually pretty unstable and depressed, despite never having attempted to find a therapist or develop any heathy coping mechanisms. This usually makes for a good comedian, but Daniel seemed to be a special case.

Damsel loved him anyway, which meant one thing and one thing only—the Curse had been broken.

Damsel rejoiced! Her Court of Admirers rejoiced! The crying woman rejoiced! The other crying woman rejoiced! The angry couple were too busy fighting to rejoice, but Damsel knew they would rejoice if they could! Daniel rejoiced (he was rejoicing over a meme he saw on Instagram, but still)! Damsel's mother rejoiced because grandchildren finally seemed like a possibility! All around, there was much, much, much rejoicing.

As the entire kingdom rejoiced, they failed to see something darker, more twisted, brewing on the horizon. You see, Damsel may have broken her Curse of One Criterion, but she was not free. No, quite the opposite, indeed.

She now had a new Curse. The Curse of Fixing Him.

What I Want to Do with the Question besides "Pop" It

- Await it

- Inquire as to its arrival

- Announce it

- Bop it

- Twist it

- Pull it

- Demand it

- Lie there. Oh, sorry, I thought you were asking about sex again.

- Question it

- Stay up all night, completely distraught with uncertainty regarding it

- Assert it

- Fart in its general direction

- Discuss it extensively—is it really the type of thing you want to surprise your partner with? You've all lost your minds!

- Stroke it, if it comes to that

- Ask it? Maybe, someday.

If you enjoy this, please see my follow-up think piece: *Knots I Tied on My Sneakers to Practice for Tying "The Knot,"* and my follow-up to that: *Can Anybody Help Me Untie These Knots, I Can't Get My Shoes Off.*

Stay Close to Friends Who Have Settled Down with Their Pet Rocks

Growing up is difficult. We all reach adulthood at different points. For some of us, it's when we go to college, but for anyone normal, it's late twenties to early forties. Like most young women, I saw a lot of my friendships starting to change at that awkward age where my friends settled down with their pet rocks. When my third friend let a piece of granite eat at the table with us, I thought things would never be fun again, but I realized I was wrong. I've learned a ton about how to keep my friendships intact in the face of personal growth, and I wanted to share some advice.

Acknowledge that friendships change when you get older.
I know it feels like yesterday that you and all your girlfriends were dancing on tables at Sigma Chi together. You still think fondly of the days when "on the rocks" meant "ice" and not that Tina's pet rock was paying for dinner (really sweet of Fluffy), but you have to acknowledge that people change. Just because your college BFF spends Saturday nights with her pet rock doesn't necessarily mean she's delusional.

Enjoy the perks of having friends with pet rocks. Having
friends with pet rocks can be great; you get all the fun of owning a pet rock with none of the responsibility! For example, the other day I visited my friend Katie and her pet rock, Stevie. I was scared I'd drop Stevie, but she assured me that it was okay to drop it because it's a rock ("it" was her pronoun, not mine). Stevie was in a great mood because it hadn't missed its nap. Because it's a rock. So it's never not asleep.

Suggest pet rock–friendly activities for the group. Don't
invite your friends to the beach to skip stones. This is insensitive to those hoping to bring their rocks along.

Don't make a point of how different your lives are now. Your friends know they've changed since they got pet rocks. You don't need to point this out by reminding them that you don't consider something a pet unless it breathes. Remember that time you kept your dead gerbil in your freezer? This is like that. But don't tell them you think so.

Be open about the social stigma of being rock-free. A lot of women face social pressure to get a pet rock, particularly from their partners. When I was giving birth to my second child, my husband looked me straight in the eyes and said, "Sweetheart, are you ready to commit to a pet rock?" As I gazed deeply at the man I'd promised to spend my life with, while I expelled a second human being from me, I said, "I'm in labor right now, can we talk about this another time?"

No matter how supportive your partner is, do not refer to him or her as your "rock." If you call the people you love rocks, this minimizes the feelings of people who actually love rocks. Also, if a friend loses their pet rock, don't try to relate by talking about how you accidentally kicked a rock into a gutter once.

Stand up for yourself when your friends try to rock-shame you. The other day, I posted an Instagram of my youngest daughter coughing up phlegm and captioned it "cleaning up phlegm #adulting." Do you know what my friend Tracy did? She commented, "You won't even know what #adulting is until you get a pet rock." As if a pet rock is the only path to maturity and life satisfaction! I told her that I can live a perfectly happy, satisfying life without one. It's the little things I love, like cooking, knitting, yoga, my extremely successful and lucrative career, and raising four children.

Make new friends. This is important. As nice as it is to hang on to your old friends, you want to make sure you have some friends who don't have pet rocks. This way, you *can* go to the beach to skip rocks, from time to time, as long as you don't post about it on social media. And if your new friends start adopting pet rocks themselves, ask yourself why all your friends are prone to adopting inanimate objects. Maybe the problem is you.

(originally seen on vulture.com)

The Hands on My Biological Clock

I wish even *one person* had told me to keep in mind that women stop being able to get pregnant at some point. Oh, right, it's all anybody ever talks about once you hit, I don't know, twenty-three? twenty-one? twelve? Our bodies have not kept pace with society. Thirty is the new twenty; sweet sixteens should happen at age thirty-two when we've finally figured out our most flattering haircut, and I shouldn't have to think about whether or not my thirty-six-year-old first date who considers scrolling Instagram "reading" would make a good father. Where can I fill out an extension request form for my fertility? Until then, the hands on my biological clock keep ticking, following a time line that goes something like this:

Noon: You think I can have a kid? I *am* a kid!

1 p.m.: Laughed out loud when the gynecologist asked if a five-year IUD was too long. Do they make fifteen-year ones? I'd like two of those.

2 p.m.: Scrolled past photos of my cousin's new baby. Felt nothing. No offense to the baby—he's fine.

3 p.m.: Nervously realized I can count on one hand the number of years to my thirtieth birthday. Considered having several fingers removed.

4 p.m.: Read one article about egg-freezing but had to stop in the middle because my partner at the time wanted me to watch *Shallow Hal*, which he considered "art."

5 p.m.: Considered having my IUD removed. Tried to book an appointment online, but they told me I'd have to make a phone call. Not worth it—I'll just let it expire.

6 p.m.: Went on a date with a man who described marriage as "jail." Temporarily jumped back to the early afternoon. Replaced my IUD with a new one, as I realized that I don't need to raise children when I can just raise the guys I date (and educate them about the criminal justice system).

7 p.m.: Wondered if that person I rejected when I was twenty-three—the one who said their number one dream in life was to be a parent—is still single.

7:02 p.m.: Googled them. They're married. Had meltdown. Ate mac 'n' cheese.

8 p.m.: Muted every parent on Instagram. Babies are becoming hard to look at. Why didn't anyone warn me about this biological clock thing? Why do I have to "feel things"?

9 p.m.: Deleted my Tinder because I came to realize it's not for serious dating. Changed my OkCupid bio to "Looking for something serious, interested in starting a family." Got 80 percent fewer matches. Told my therapist, who said that was okay, because I was just filtering for what I wanted. Changed my bio back to "I think farts are funny" (I do).

10 p.m.: Started a savings fund.

11 p.m.: Saw a toddler in public and had a full-blown meltdown. It was literally walking that way—the little waddle—to manipulate me. Why did it have such big eyes? It can't even read.

11:30 p.m.: Stayed up all night reading about egg-freezing.

11:45 p.m.: Made simultaneous appointments at an adoption agency and a fertility clinic.

Midnight: Reactivated my Tinder and immediately matched with a skateboarder. This is a disaster.

The Aforementioned Extension Request for My Fertility

1. **Request:** Dear Creator (whoever you are—sorry for saying I didn't believe in you, although, to be honest, I still don't), I was wondering if I could maybe have my biological clock reprogrammed. You see, I'm nearing thirty-five, and I've been repeatedly told I'm about to dry up like a kale chip any day now. As such, I'd like to formally request an extension on my fertility.

2. **Description of Extenuating Circumstances:** It's not about me at all, it's just the people I date. You see, I date men who use dish soap as shampoo, so I'm not really approaching any sort of "ready." I also can't get a crib as I'm boycotting Amazon for progressive reasons (at least, my crush liked several anti-Amazon tweets, so now I'm on board, too). I'm also way too young to have a child. I don't even have my own Netflix account (what will Baby watch?). Okay, so I guess it's also sort of about me.

3. **Technical Specifications:** Yes, there's currently a way to get an extension on fertility, but it's very expensive and involves needles. You don't want me to get poked and go broke, do you? So I was thinking we could strike a bargain—for every ten people I swipe through on Hinge, I get one more fertile egg, but it just shows up automatically, like a refund? That seems like a good incentive structure (I majored in economics, thirteen years ago).

4. **Proposed Due Date:** Could I have another twenty years? I haven't even started *Game of Thrones*, so I'm sure that'll take me out of the game for a year or so, and then I need to learn how to cook—another two. Move out of my mom's basement—another year. Emotionally mature to the point where I feel ready to raise kids—fifteen years. So I could actually have it done for you in . . . nineteen years? Would that work?

5. **Opportunities Afforded by the Extension:** Well, like so many women my age, an extension on my fertility gives me a chance to really lean into my career without worrying about having a child. No, I personally doubt I'll use this time to do so, but I *could* if I wanted to. And that's not to say I won't take advantage of them in my own way. I'll likely use the remaining fertile years to experiment with more types of birth control until I find the one that makes me cry on the exact same schedule as my best friend Sheila, so we can plan girls' night a bit more easily. Plus, I'll be able to continue dating as I've been doing, which isn't necessarily good for me, but it is good for Brooklinen, as I've persuaded eight different guys to buy their top sheets.

6. **Positive Social Externalities:** I can't provide any specifics, but you do *not* want my straight female friends who are also around age thirty-five to raise kids with the guys they're with now. Unless you look around the world and think, We really need more LARPers.

7. **Steps to Take to Ensure Proposed Due Date Will Be Sufficient:** Who are you, my mother, all my aunts, my Instagram feed, and society? I'll be ready when I'm ready.

8. **Completed Work to Be Submitted:** A baby, I guess. That actually brings me to my next request—could I have a girl, please? I just can't with men.

Cost-Effective Replacements for Weddings

Do you know why people cry at weddings? Because they're mourning the loss of their friendship with the betrothed. While this isn't 100 percent true (I mean, it's definitely *sometimes* true), why is this—relative to so many other important life stages—the one we all gather for? The idea that a wedding is a must-have event in the life of a relationship feels just a bit outdated. In my opinion, we should be able to celebrate love without throwing a wildly expensive party—possibly via one of the following:

- A big party with no vows

- Gathering all your friends and doing the Macarena

- Asking friends to each create six new Instagram accounts so that your engagement pic gets over 3,000 likes. (If you have that many friends. Personally, I think three is plenty. Friends, not likes.)

- Having all your friends plant one tree in your honor

- Making everyone get you gifts without planning a party

- Getting an entire week of calling your fiancé "bae" online without anyone unfollowing you

- Having all your exes watch your Instagram story at once

- A really nice back massage. Ninety minutes, at least. And when I say "back," I'm also including the bottom of your feet.

- Setting a big pile of money on fire in front of all your loved ones, and laughing as it burns

- Another season of *Fleabag*

- An open bar, anywhere on the planet. If this isn't possible, two bags of Franzia and a pair of scissors will do.

- A Zoom where everyone is muted and you get to tell all your friends, in lurid detail, about the best sex you and your fiancé have ever had and *then* you get to tell them all, in lurid detail, about how your PMS symptoms this cycle vary slightly from last cycle

- A gift card to Olive Garden, but, like, a *big* one

What May Happen If I Don't Lose My Absolute Shit Over Someone Else's Baby

According to all your mother's friends, babies should be on your mind every time you open the Hinge app, because honestly—they should be on your mind constantly. In fact, if a woman deigns to let you see her baby, you must fall to your knees and break down in tears at how beautiful and perfect the child is. It's a *child*. A *baby*. And regardless of whether or not you personally want to have your own child, you must worship—with prayers and sacrifices and goats—at the altar of any infant you see, because looking at a nine-month-old take a shit is truly a once-in-a-lifetime opportunity. And if you don't . . .

- The mother will say, "Wait, you're not obsessed with *my* baby?! It's a *baby*."

- Everyone on the street will freeze exactly where they are upon hearing such a ghastly statement.

- Every person within a three-mile radius will suddenly surround you in a moblike fashion. How did they get there? No one knows. It's one of life's many mysteries, like "Where do babies come from?"

- In unison, the women will chant, "Did you just *ignore* this *baby*!?!"

- One will eye you suspiciously and ask if you want to be *alone forever*. Indeed, it is your inability to exalt a small child that has caused your single-hood—not your own personal decision to be single.

- Your two deceased great-aunts will return to Earth to join in the inquisition. They will excoriate you for not adoring the child. They will not take questions about whether they ended up in Heaven or Hell. You will make a note to ask them later.

- You will respond to the angry crowd. "I didn't ignore her, I just waved for a second and then returned to my phone—"

- It will be too late.

- One—the group leader—will ask what could be more important than a baby. She'll demand to know if you *hated* the child.

- You will begin to explain that you're a trauma surgeon, and you were busy receiving an update on a patient, but before you can say "trauma—"

- It's inflicted on you. And the weapon of choice? A used diaper—the scent of champions.

- You'll think about feminism, and why all those women sacrificed, only for you—a thirty-two-year-old, successful doctor—to be pressured into cooing at any tiny infant you encounter and genuflect in the presence of a partner who wants to reproduce with you.

- The baby will start to cry. Oh, no. There's truly nothing in the world more devastating than making a *baby* cry. They only do it every two hours. The situation is far beyond repair. There's only one option . . .

- Yes. They've wheeled out the stake. They must burn you. As they're tying you up, about to light you on fire, you say—

- "Wait! I think I'm ovulating. And my partner and I—we were going to start trying."

- They set you free, to make love. Your partner doesn't exist, but far be it for any of these women to deprive the world of another *baby*. Besides, at thirty-two, they know you won't have that many more chances.

- You will wonder how they know you're thirty-two. You may touch your forehead self-consciously.

- You'll take another look at the baby. And you think, It's a little cute . . . but also . . . a little weird-looking. Like, kind of lumpy.

- Some babies are *super* weird-looking.

What I'll Miss If I Get Married

An easy way to give any story a happy ending is to have the female protagonist get married (the *Little Women* phenomenon). And I'll admit that I, too, have fantasized about one day having a spouse or, at the very least, someone to do my taxes. But singlehood isn't so bad. It's important to remind myself of everything I'd be giving up.

- That five-day window between when a man decides he'd like to have sex with me and when he does, during which he is extremely attentive to my needs

- Having my friends speculate on when I'll tie the knot. This is annoying, but it also means the conversation is focused on me, which I like.

- My parents' cell phone plan. I assume I have to get my own when I get married, but my current strategy is to never bring it up, and hope they don't notice I'm still on it.

- Strangers expressing shock that I'm not married. No, this doesn't happen, but it could.

- My perennial pastime of deciding who gets invited to the wedding

- The chance to meet an exciting new guy. Indeed, after marriage, I'll likely delete Sea Captain Date.

- Reading studies about how being unmarried makes you happier. I will now have to switch to exclusively reading studies about how being married makes you happier. Science is a delight.

- Not sounding like a boomer when I talk about dating apps

- The ability to express open excitement that an old crush watched my Instagram story. I'll still have it, I just can't say it. I don't think.

- Using the phrase "this idiot," and having people know I think the person is an actual idiot, it's not just me trying to be cutesy on Valentine's Day

- The rush of hope when a celebrity comes into my travel bookstore (*Notting Hill* was based on a true story, just not one that's happened yet)

- Passing gas in my own bed without disdain or comment

- Wondering who I'll fall in love with

- Wondering who I'll end up with

- Wondering who I'll settle for

- Loudly reminding everyone that most marriages end in divorce. I guess I could keep doing this, just not when my partner is in the room.

- Clean air. This isn't related to marriage, we just have less and less of it every year.

- A good excuse for not having kids

- A good excuse for not buying a house

- Oh, wait, this economy is a good excuse for both of those.

- Explaining to casual acquaintances that I actually *can* see my life without marriage because I'm fulfilled in other ways. For example, you don't have to be married to enjoy cheese or find your career meaningful. You don't have to get married to have a family or a community of people to spend your life with or a hot tub, and being unmarried doesn't mean you're alone. Besides, being alone is sort of nice—I'm making great progress on my goal of watching YouTube. Plus, it's possible to get married at any point in your adult life—maybe I'll try it in my sixties. That sounds nice.

- The fun I had as a single woman. I liked my life.

Deciding
TO BE
SINGLE
·IF·
YOU
WANT

If we're constantly asking single people when they intend to get married, we may as well start asking married people when they plan to get divorced. Of course, I don't actually wish divorce on anyone, unless they want to, in which case, I'm very pro.

Much like with relationships, I resent that the default assumption is that everyone wants to get married, or that marriage is some sort of culmination of a relationship. I'm not going to lie—I've imagined myself married to anyone I've gone on more than two dates with, and many with whom I haven't even gotten that far. This would probably unsettle them to hear, but it's even more unsettling to me—I don't think I even want to get married. It feels like voluntary paperwork, and I hate the idea that a social construct would keep me and my partner together longer than either of us wanted. Of course, this opinion is subject to change in the event that someone asks me, but still.

Time isn't free. Time spent in relationships is time you could be spending with your family or traveling or working toward a promotion or learning how to juggle. I could probably have three PhDs by now if I'd never downloaded Tinder, although my friends with PhDs disagree and also find that statement offensive.

And even *if* marriage itself weren't a bureaucratic hassle and even *if* relationships didn't take up time and even *if* they didn't come with a million and a half downsides that we've explored so far, I could still just not want one. Even the easiest relationship in the world. I could decide it's not for me, and that would be fine. And if you feel that way too, you're allowed. You can just prefer being single. Because remember—like my mother always said, the easiest way to avoid getting married to a dude named Chad is to not get married at all.

My Life as a Single Woman, According to All My Friends in Relationships

The best part of being single in your late twenties is that all your friends are starting to get engaged and you're not. It's really charming to watch their lives advance in a conventional trajectory while yours, you know, goes on. My friends in relationships seem to take pity on me, but they're not seeing the best parts of singlehood—I don't have to keep my apartment clean, I can sleep with a twenty-two-year-old if I want, and I don't have to promote anyone's podcast but my own. They have their own idea of my lonely life, though, and it looks a little something like this:

- All I want is a nice partner who then becomes my spouse.

- I'm, like, so cute, but I need my friends to remind me because I don't have anyone else to do it. I sell myself short. A lot.

- My friends don't understand how I'm still single!

- My friends *sort of* understand how I'm still single.

- I really shouldn't beat myself up about still being single (Note: I don't beat myself up, and I don't use the phrase "still single").

- Every time I put mascara on, my intention is to attract someone.

- I'm just ready to get off this insane hamster wheel known as dating. I'm definitely not enjoying the free food and meeting tons of new people.

- I stay in shape, so it just really makes no sense to me why I don't have at *least* one ring.

- I only stay in shape to get at least one ring.

- I'm extremely envious of all my friends in relationships, even if all they do is fight with their partners.

- My thirtieth birthday will be the worst day of my life.

- I would be such a catch, if only I acted like all my married friends in every way.

- I look forward to finding a spouse so I can start eating carbs again.

- I've used every single dating app. Literally, every last one. I paid a photographer to take photos of me for my most recent Hinge profile. I took money out of my 401k to do that. It seemed worthwhile—all my friends told me it was.

- I'm so bored of my vibrator.

- I'm not offended when someone suggests I use a $5,000 per year matchmaking service. It's a great idea! Who needs a 401k?

- I sleep around, and I *hate* it.

- I'm so lucky to have so many married friends to set a good example for me.

- I read the *New York Times* Modern Love column every Sunday with a box of tissues nearby.

- My life won't feel complete until I have a partner/fiancé/spouse/rat infestation. Just something so that I'm no longer alone. I'm so alone.

- I am so *grateful* to anyone who offers to set me up, even if he's twelve years my senior and thrice-divorced.

- I have a device installed to drink white wine in my shower. I'd prefer to shower with a partner, but white wine fills the void. I don't think the idea of having a partner in the shower sounds remotely inconvenient or inefficient. Without one, I have no choice but to shower, drink, and cry.

- I'm way too picky for how long I've been single. I should be happy with a loaf of bread (not to eat—to marry. No carbs until I'm married!).

- Whenever a new friend of mine gets engaged, I sob.

- I only go on Facebook to see other people's happiness and burst into tears.

- I'm extremely aware that all my friends feel sorry for me, and I feel bad for making them pity me! They shouldn't have to deal with this—my singlehood is my fault and mine alone. This makes me cry.

- I nervously check my calendar every six minutes to watch my eggs slowly die. As I do, I wet myself (with tears). Also, yes, I have a calendar that tells me how fast my eggs are dying. It was a kind gift from my most recently married friend.

- The last time I was truly happy was in my last relationship, with my boyfriend, Tad, who cheated on me with my sister. God, I wish I could get him back. (Cue a tear dramatically rolling down my already-tearstained cheek.)

- I need to have faith. There's at least one right person for me out there, and I will have value as a human once I meet them. I need to put down the tissue boxes that I tape to my tits for easy access, stop feeling sorry for myself, and accept literally anyone who looks my way.

- I'm so lonely.

Above all, my friends in relationships believe I have this fun quirk where I like to insist I'm happy being single. I'm happy being single.

(originally seen on mcsweeneys.net)

Avoid Being Unsingle

If you're anything like me, you've seen your poor friends go through a breakup and then tell you that they're committed to "staying single" for the next few months. I'm such a good friend that I really do feel sorry for them in their steadfast, deliberate attempts to stave off impending relationships. However, it's never been my struggle because, not to brag, I'm actually *effortlessly* single.

Unsingles are super jealous of me, which I know, because every time I see my unsingle friends, all they want to do is swipe through profiles on my Hinge account. (Why do people in relationships always want to use dating apps?) Anyway, if you, too, are looking for advice on how to avoid being unsingle, I'm here to help.

Break Up with Any Current Partners. Yes, if you're currently unsingle and want a way out, you need to call it quits on your relationship. Do it via public comment on their Facebook post if you want to avoid a situation in which they ever try to make you unsingle again.

Update Your Technology. You must get rid of your dating apps, or else you risk being drawn back into unsingledom. Apple makes it difficult to delete things, so I recommend ceremoniously throwing your iPhone into the sea. You can also try to get yourself banned from Hinge by pretending to be Lucy Liu. In my experience, this works about 70 percent of the time.

Be Frugal. Companies sell tons of products attempting to teach women how to stay single—Postmates, Netflix, aluminum-free deodorant, etc. It's capitalism at its worst, trying to get women hooked on the idea that they need to spend a ton of money to be alone. I have good news—I've never invested one single dollar in being single, and yet I haven't been touched in seven years. Simply spend zero dollars on anything—including the gas or bus fare needed to get to a date—and boom—eternally single.

Hit the Gym. If you have plans with a potential partner, go to the gym instead. If you're supposed to be at a party socializing, go to the gym instead. Jury duty? Skip it for the gym. What you do at the gym is none of my business—I like to scroll Instagram in the steam room and sometimes steal toilet paper—but what's important is that you *actively turn down romantic opportunities* in your life to be *at* the gym.

Location Location Location. Specifically, your couch. Staying inside the home at all times comes effortlessly to me, but with a little practice and a lot of takeout, you, too, can avoid all romantic entanglements by parking yourself on your couch. My only warning is that you not give in to temptation and use the time at home as a reason to deep-clean your apartment. Letting a layer of filth set in will detract matches and help you stay happily single!

Avoid Matt. He wants to date you. I can tell. Steer clear.

Communicate Effectively. Did you receive one text from a potential love interest today? Send them 197 back. As Stephen King once said, the road to hell is paved with adverbs; and, as I always say, the road to singledom is paved with 4,000-word Instagram DMs. This strategy has worked for me in the past, present, and future.

Be Yourself. This doesn't work for everything, but for me personally, it's a foolproof way to avoid unsinglehood.

♫ *Maybe it's me, or maybe it's the fact that I brought my mom on our first date.* ♫

The Annual Progression of My Dating Goals

Like many of you, I began this year thinking I'd find the love of my life. Or, at least, a person to have sex with. I started off as ambitious as anyone else, and I'm proud to tell you that I did, indeed, find great joy. Here's how my goals evolved throughout the year:

January: Go on one date a week. Use dating apps, ask friends to set you up, even venture into the world if you're feeling particularly bold (which you're not). Just try something.

February: Go on one date every other week.

March: Ask one person per month to hang out. It's okay if I only do this in March.

April: Start a conversation with a new person on a dating app every week.

May: Match with one new person a week.

June: Respond to at least one message on Hinge per month.

July: Swipe right on at least one person at least once a month.

August: Swipe one time on any app, including Grubhub.

September: Open one dating app one time.

October: Make eye contact with someone attractive in a public place at least once before this year is over.

November: Think about the possibility of thinking about the possibility of dating.

December: Realize you're happier single. Enjoy the holidays.

Late December: Remember that no one enjoys the holidays.

My Group Text Chain When I Say I'm Not Looking for a Relationship

Kaitlyn:

G—can I set you up with my friend Matt! He's single

Me:

What's he like?

Zara:

I've met Matt. He's single. He's neither married nor engaged nor raising kids. He had a partner for a while, but now he doesn't. He's super single. Like, so single it's hard to imagine him in a relationship. He's perfect for you.

Me:

Is he cool?

Kaitlyn:

He's single

Me:

Do you know if he's looking for a relationship?

Kaitlyn:

Yeah.

Me:

He said that?

Zara:

He's not in a relationship. He's looking.

Vicky:
LOL

Me:
What?

Vicky:
NVM, just Gr8ful for this thread

Me:
Thanks, but I think I'll pass on Matt

Kaitlyn:
Why?? I said he's single!! And you're single. I don't see the issue.

Zara:
Don't you want to be fixed?

Me:
Do you mean fixed up?

Zara:
No, I mean fixed

Me:
I actually like being single

Vicky:
LOL

Me:
What?

(Two hours pass.)

Kaitlyn:
Wait, what? I had to digitally detox because my boyfriend said I seemed scattered.

Zara:
You're so lucky to have a guy around to fix you

Kaitlyn:
Speaking of, I can text Matt. I want to set you up, G. You'll like him.

Vicky:

You go girl!!! I love this plan

Kaitlyn:

Who was that directed at?

Zara:

I just asked Matt, you guys now have dinner plans Wednesday

Kaitlyn:

Ok so girls' night Thursday to debrief

Me:

I like that I get to watch whatever TV show I want, I like that I get my whole bed to myself—it helps me sleep better. I like that I set my own schedule, and I don't have to deal with someone else's friends or family. I'm not lonely, and it's not that I never want to date, it's just not what I'm looking for right now.

Zara:

Oh, the conversation has moved on.

Kaitlyn:

The dangers of sending a long text to a group chat

Has G lost her MIND!?!?

Omg, meant to send that just to Zara

So annoying how when you search someone's name in iMessage, the group chat comes up before the one-on-one conversation

Vicky:

Yaaasssssss

Me:

No worries, but I haven't lost my mind. I am busy, though—I just got promoted!

Zara:

What's the joy in getting a promotion when you have no one to share it with?

Me:

I'm sharing it with you guys

Zara:

Ok but you know what I mean

Me:

I don't

Kaitlyn:

We just want you to be happy

Me:

I am happy

Zara:

Ya but like happy in a real, fulfilling, sustainable way that you can tell people about

Kaitlyn:

And you don't have to pretend around us. It's ok to admit you hate being single

Me:

I don't hate being single

Kaitlyn:

You'll like matt. He's also horny

UGH autocorrect, sorry. I meant to say he's also always in a good mood and a Capricorn

Me:

I don't believe that was autocorrect

Vicky:

Get it

Kaitlyn:

I feel like Vicky's not paying attention to the text convo

Vicky:

LOL

Kaitlyn:

Oops sorry I thought that was a one-on-one again

G—don't you want the security of knowing someone likes you?

Me:

A lot of people like me.

Kaitlyn:

You know what I mean.

Me:

I don't.

Zara:

Gaaahhhhh did you guys see Matt's Insta?

Downloading
JPG 340 MGB

Kaitlyn:

What???

Zara:

He just got engaged

He got engaged!?!? So he had a serious partner this whole time? And you wanted to set me up with him? We had a date scheduled for Wednesday!

Kaitlyn:

Yeah but he wasn't ENGAGED.

Zara:

We thought you still had a shot

Vicky:

LOL

Terrible Things That Will Happen If You're Single at Thirty

There's only one day that separates being twenty-nine from being thirty, but society's managed to imbue age thirty with a certain kind of morbid importance. Fun (and untrue) fact: If you're single the day you turn thirty, your status actually changes to "drastically single," no matter what else is going on in your life. In the event that you find yourself absolutely and 100 percent alone at age thirty, surrounded only by large swaths of loving friends and family, the following may befall you:

- You can go on many dates with many different people. Most of them will be fascinating and delightful and pay for your meal and greatly enrich your life. However, one of them will leave a banana peel on the floor of your apartment, and you'll slip on it.

- You don't have children to get home to, so following a long day of earning big money, you get a back massage. However, the masseuse uses a different kind of lotion, and you now have a rash on your back. Because you're scratching your back on the walk home, you're not paying attention, and you slip on a banana peel on the street.

- You have many vacation days since you didn't use any going to visit your spouse's uncle in Arkansas (spouses always seem to have uncles in Arkansas). You decide to take a soothing trip to Thailand. It's beautiful, and you return so relaxed that you stop worrying about little things like cleaning fruit rinds off the floor of your apartment. Oops—that peel was pretty slippery.

- You sleep through the night, because there's no one to wake you up (you also took a Tylenol PM, on account of the back pain, from the fall). Your sleep is so healthy that you don't even toss when someone breaks into your apartment to leave behind a banana peel, on which you will slip. Fortunately, the prior falls taught you a lesson, and you now walk around with pillows strapped to you. Comfy!

- You win an award for just killing it at life. However, when you stand up to receive it, you realize you can't walk that easily, on account of the pillows, on account of the banana peel. You sit back down. Hank accepts the award for you, which is fitting, since he takes all credit for everything else you've done, too.

- Undistracted by a romantic partner, your mind is completely at peace. You smile at random strangers, which leads them to believe you're on drugs. So then they offer you more drugs. So then, you actually *are* on drugs, and you don't notice the banana peel betwixt your feet.

- Your life is so filled with friendship, professional satisfaction, personal relationships, a house with a working dishwasher and a window (the millennial dream), and independence. Sure, you've lost some friends along the way. ("Why don't you just stop leaving banana peels on the floor of your apartment?" Ronna said. Ronna is dead to you.) You're completely content and so financially stable you don't even care that you keep slipping on stray banana peels. By the way, who is littering this much? Wait—is someone intentionally following you around with banana peels, trying to make you fall? You become extremely paranoid.

- You eventually go to a therapist to seek treatment for the banana-peel-induced paranoia. While you're there, you run into your friend Sally, who's been happily married for six years. "What are you doing here?" you ask Sally. She says, "I'm suffering from banana-peel-induced paranoia." *What.* You didn't realize it was something that could happen to people in relationships, too. You thought this was punishment for being single at thirty. Your worldview is shattered.

- You eat a banana. You throw the peel in the trash, but you miss, and it lands on the ground. You're single—no one can tell you what to do in your apartment. The cycle begins anew.

How I Might Otherwise Have Filled the Time I Spent Trying to Find a Partner

- Calling my friends

- Gardening

- Baking bread. No, I don't seem like a woman who'd successfully bake bread, but maybe I *could have been* if I'd had more free time.

- Wearing matching socks. This was a huge emotional commitment I didn't have the bandwidth for when I was getting ghosted a lot.

- Rereading *Lord of the Rings*. Five times *wasn't* enough.

- Waiting for things to happen when I least expected them. Indeed, I spent most of my twenties least expecting things, and yet . . . it didn't happen.

- Picking out the perfect vibrator. Like, the *perfect* one. One I can be with forever.

- Becoming an avid Reddit user. Actually, maybe it's good I didn't do this.

- Thinking about what I really want in my career

- Thinking about what I really want in a relationship

- Thinking about whether or not I really want a relationship

- Thinking about whether or not Brad Pitt regrets his choices. (He does.)

- Thinking about things

- Thinking

- More thinking. I did some thinking—but I wish I'd had the time to think . . . more.

- Therapy. I mean, I did this the whole time, but I would have spent more time, you know, thinking about what my therapist said after the appointment. And possibly if I'd thought more about what she said, I wouldn't have kept sleeping with Brad. My bad.

- Getting to know myself well enough that when or if someone I like comes along, I can determine whether *they* fit into *my* life, not the other way around. My therapist told me this was important (see, I did listen to *some* of what she said).

- It's not that I never did any of these things, it's that I would have done them all a lot more. And it's not that I think hunting for a partner was entirely a waste of time—I learned some things about myself, and I met some . . . interesting people. It's more that I didn't really need to make it one of my *central* goals; I could have waited to see if I found someone who effortlessly fit into my life, instead of always feeling like I was on the hunt. But, to be fair, I did several of the things I just mentioned. My vibrator is pretty good; okay, I'll give it that.

- Napping. Dating is exhausting.

Conclusion

Congratulations on finishing this book! I'm sorry to say that the time you spent reading it was time you could have spent swiping through dating apps trying to find "The One." However, I'm happy to say that reading this book was probably a better use of your time. (I hope!) Can you even imagine if reading this were less fun than dating, an activity that we just spent 231 pages unpacking and proving is notoriously laborious and unpleasant?

Like I said earlier, I was single for most of my twenties. What I wanted more than a partner was to stop feeling self-conscious about my singledom. I worried I stuck out like a sore thumb at parties and weddings where I was among very few single people. But then I remembered something profound a friend once said: "I've never noticed anyone else's sore thumb." It's true. Dating is something you should really only do for yourself.

I started writing this book in March 2020. As you may remember, it was not the most significant event to happen in March 2020 (that would have to be the launch of the podcast "Last Degree of Kevin Bacon," followed by the spread of the global coronavirus pandemic). I thought I couldn't get any more single than I was, and then the country shut down. It turns out that the only thing worse than getting within six feet of your weird Tinder date is not having the opportunity to get within six feet of your weird Tinder date.

I had several long months of complete isolation to reflect on my love life. I'd had what you might call "a lot of ups and downs," which is an expression reserved for times when there are vastly more downs than ups. I assumed there was something wrong with me, that I alone was unable to make a relationship work. Dating felt sadistic, so why keep going? We were all stuck inside, so it seemed moot, anyway.

At some point, the loneliness overwhelmed me and I re-downloaded Hinge. I wasn't hopeful—I felt like I was doing it because I thought I "should," much like I'd been doing for the last decade, or like I had to because people felt sorry for me for being all alone in a pandemic. Also, I was bored. So bored. Like, rewatching–*Zoey-101*–levels of bored.

Dating is a moving target, as I've mentioned many times. We're forced to stay sharp as we relearn how to date again and again, which is why single people are smarter (jk). As a teenager, I never expected I'd do most of my dating via apps, and at the start of 2020 I never expected it'd get even weirder and I'd date wearing a face mask. But it did, and I did.

As you may have guessed, I met someone. (That's typically the way stories work: You introduce an unlikely event, then you do a lot of buildup, then you reveal that the unlikely event came to pass—please sign up for my master class.) And he was nice, and it was simple. It wasn't like my past romantic encounters. I didn't have to shoehorn him into my life or badger him about commitment. And all of a sudden, after reaching peak solitude during lockdown, I wasn't alone anymore.

It was so easy I briefly wondered if I was "settling"—a millennial's last words. After years of the evasive commitment-phobes, I thought it should feel like a huge accomplishment when you get someone to be in a relationship with you—and huge accomplishments take work and persistence, like how I finished four seasons of *Zoey 101* despite desperately wanting not to (It's also not on streaming. I literally bought the episodes for $0.99 each).

But it didn't feel like an accomplishment because relationships aren't supposed to be accomplishments. You're not better for being in one; you've just picked that lifestyle and found someone you're compatible with it. It's not unlike brewing your own kombucha—you have to just decide you're going to do it (I say this having never successfully brewed my own kombucha, but you get the idea). I'd worried so much that I, Ginny, the Person, was humanly incapable of being in a relationship. But one day, I didn't have a boyfriend; and the next day, I did. I was no different.

It's not wholly accurate to say I spent all of my twenties single. I actually devoted a great deal of time to the very start of relationships. And I could barely enjoy these budding relationships. I was preoccupied with worrying about when they would end because, in my experience, the end was imminent. Each date would feel like the next step in an interview process for a job that I could get fired from any day.

But I didn't feel that way about my boyfriend because he never tried to be evasive, and the future was so out of sight anyway. We didn't know when we'd next be able to leave our city; what was the point in planning, anyway? After months of isolation, having someone to make dinner with while watching *Gilmore Girls* (I'd upgraded) was the ultimate luxury, especially when you factor in our division of labor—he made dinner, I watched *Gilmore Girls*.

During the pandemic, I felt grateful for any day when I wasn't miserable. If our newfound romance ended, that was okay—I had still gotten a break from the solitude.

For the first time, I let go of the idea that my relationship was supposed to offer me stability—I couldn't put the responsibility of stabilizing a chaotic world on him. And what remained, when I'd abandoned some nebulous idea of what the future should be, was the present where I was happy. Isn't that so dumb, that it took me over a decade to start evaluating things by whether or not they make me happy?

Nothing about that is unique to a relationship—you can find happiness anywhere. I can't say I'm happier in a relationship than I am when I'm single, in the same way I can't say I'm happier lying down than sitting up. It depends on the couch. Actually, I'm happier lying down (this analogy has failed).

And then – unsurprising plot twist – the relationship ended. And I was happier after it ended, maybe because I also moved cities, became an aunt, got vaccinated against COVID, started an exciting new project, and began eating prebiotics. My happiness could be attributed to any of these things (but let's face it – it's probably the prebiotics). In that breakup, I found joy in being single. Which isn't to say I'll never again find joy in a relationship – more so that I can't stake my happiness on it. A relationship can't "fix" me, and I wouldn't want it to because then I'd feel dependent.

I'm not going to tell you to "learn to love yourself" (or whatever), whether or not you're in a relationship. That's the worst advice of all time, and I don't actually know how you're supposed to do that.

I'm also not going to tell you to stop dating if it doesn't bring you constant joy. I generally find the "Why do it if it's not fun for you" line of reasoning annoying and a little out-of-touch. I love drinking coffee, but I'm not going to pretend it doesn't give me panic attacks after the fourth cup. Not every day can be spectacularly perfect, but I think that if even a small fraction of each day is comprised of joy and fun, that's a good day. You don't have to find every moment of dating fun to consider the experience worthwhile—it's entirely up to you.

And I'm not going to tell you that no one thinks differently of you when you're in a relationship versus when you're single. Some people do, and some people express pity toward the singles, and that sucks. But some people also think differently of you when you change your hair or move or switch careers or tweet the word "tits" seventeen times in a row (I'm still *me*, okay?). So you can't really let it derail you.

This was not an advice book, as I hope you've noticed by now (and if you haven't, I'm so sorry). I have no grand insights. I don't even have small insights (except that if you can't clean it with baking soda, don't bother. Also, I think my mom's tip about IPAs was really good and potentially worth buying this book for). My hope is that no matter where you are in your dating journey, you hang onto whatever brings you moments of joy, whether or not it's connected to your romantic life.

I really just wanted to make you laugh—or, at the very least, make you smile quietly to yourself and think, "That's kind of clever." There's much to mock about this absurd and insane experience we call "dating." I hope you enjoyed!

Acknowledgments

···

What started as a few jokes about my lackluster sex life only became the book you just read because of the people who supported me along the way. I'm very grateful to Olivia Roberts and the whole team at Chronicle for bringing this idea from inception to completion, to Liz Parker for her constant support, to Lisa Mierke and Chelsea Connors for all their unflagging help throughout the years, and to my friends and family for their advice—romantically, regarding this book, and otherwise. I'd also like to thank Emma Allen, Brian Boone, and Chris Monks for publishing the original version of several of these pieces. And, lastly, I'd like to acknowledge my "source material" (all my exes). Thanks, I guess.

About the Author

Ginny Hogan is a writer and stand-up comedian. She is a contributor for the *New Yorker,* the *New York Times*, the *Atlantic*, *Cosmo*, the *Guardian*, and *McSweeney's*. She's the author of *Toxic Femininity in the Workplace* and the Audible Original *Yes We Mustard*. You can find her on Twitter @ginnyhogan_. Actually, she's quite hard to avoid on Twitter.